Online Dispute Resolution

Online Dispute Resolution

Resolving Conflicts in Cyberspace

Ethan Katsh
Janet Rifkin

 JOSSEY-BASS
A Wiley Company
San Francisco

Published by

JOSSEY-BASS
A Wiley Company
350 Sansome St.
San Francisco, CA 94104-1342

| www.josseybass.com |

Jossey-Bass books and products are available through most bookstores. To contact Jossey-Bass directly, call (888) 378-2537, fax to (800) 605-2665, or visit our website at www.josseybass.com.

Substantial discounts on bulk quantities of Jossey-Bass books are available to corporations, professional associations, and other organizations. For details and discount information, contact the special sales department at Jossey-Bass.

We at Jossey-Bass strive to use the most environmentally sensitive paper stocks available to us. Our publications are printed on acid-free recycled stock whenever possible, and our paper always meets or exceeds minimum GPO and EPA requirements.

Library of Congress Cataloging-in-Publication Data

Katsh, M. Ethan
   Online dispute resolution : resolving conflicts in cyberspace / by Ethan Katsh and Janet Rifkin.
    p. cm.
   Includes bibliographical references and index.
   ISBN 0-7879-5676-7
   1. Dispute resolution (Law)—Automation. 2. Mediation—Automation. 3. Ombudsman—Automation. 4. Internet. I. Rifkin, Janet. II. Title.

K2390.K38   2001
347'.09'0285—dc21
                                                2001029474

FIRST EDITION
HB Printing   10 9 8 7 6 5 4 3 2 1

12973862

ро

Contents

Preface

We are extremely pleased to have been asked to write this first book about conflict and conflict resolution in cyberspace. When we were first approached about this project, our editor, Alan Rinzler, suggested that there was a growing need for a book about how to resolve disputes in cyberspace and how to use online resources to manage any kind of conflict. If we have books about conflict resolution in the workplace, in schools, in families, and in the other environments we spend time in, why shouldn't there be a book about dispute resolution in cyberspace, our most intriguing new environment? We could not agree more.

On the cover of this book is a picture of a computer keyboard with one key, the ENTER key, highlighted. This book is a creation of printing technology, but we invite you to use it to enter the intriguing, challenging, powerful, creative, and always growing environment of cyberspace. You are probably already aware that cyberspace is not conflict-free. Our goal in this book is to explain how there are also resources online to deal with these problems; resources that can even help us with problems that arise offline.

Successful societies and institutions need to have accessible mechanisms for resolving problems. Yet, we have been slow to recognize that cyberspace also needs such institutions. Rather suddenly, however, online marketplaces and other E-commerce ventures have begun to understand that they will not thrive if users feel insecure, uncertain, and anxious online. Fortunately, ODR solutions are at hand and online dispute resolution has become a growth area.

We have been concerned with the subject of online dispute resolution for much of the last five years. For many years before that, one of us (Ethan) had been studying and writing about the impact of information technologies on law, but without a specific focus on dispute resolution. His books, *The Electronic Media and the Transformation of Law* and *Law in a Digital World* were among the first to recognize that what happened online would affect our legal system in many different ways. His ideas have sparked interesting debates among legal scholars about the role of law in cyberspace, and he has been involved in many of the most interesting legal initiatives in cyberspace.

Janet Rifkin was one of the earliest participants in the Alternative Dispute Resolution (ADR) movement in the United States. Interest in ADR started growing in the 1970s, and she has participated actively in it as a practitioner, researcher, teacher, and trainer. As the founder and director of the University Mediation Project and as the University Ombudsperson, she has seen first hand how conflict can undermine and erode personal and working relationships. Having trained many people in mediation practices, she was intrigued by the idea of translating these skills into online dispute resolution practices that could assist people in managing and resolving a range of online conflicts.

This is a book neither of us could have written alone. It is a book that is a result of many discussions and conversations about how to create an appropriate and effective relationship between "online" and "dispute resolution." We have been fortunate to have been able to work with ODR entrepreneurs who are designing ODR systems, with government agencies that wish to use ODR to protect citizens, and with ADR organizations trying to understand connections between ADR and ODR. We have been enriched by our discussions and interactions with diverse firms and the many individuals who, like us, are trying to anticipate the future. In this spirit, we hope this book is useful to those who see the value of technology as a critical building block in the future of dispute resolution.

To our families
Beverly, Rebecca, Gabriel, and Gideon
and
David, Alex, and Nick

Acknowledgments

Our greatest debt is to our colleagues in the Department of Legal Studies at the University of Massachusetts who have, for many years, supported and encouraged our work. We have benefitted greatly from working in a highly collegial academic environment where ideas and suggestions flow freely and where many ideas originating with our colleagues have found their way into this book. We are particularly grateful to Alan Gaitenby, our principal colleague at the Center for Information Technology and Dispute Resolution, who has worked closely with us during the past two years and on whose shoulders many extra responsibilities fell as we worked on this book.

Our work would have been over shortly after it began if not for the support we have received from the Hewlett Foundation. We are most grateful to Steve Toben, Stephanie Smith, and the Board of the Hewlett Foundation for understanding that dispute resolution, a process that typically occurred with parties meeting face to face, would be affected deeply as conflict occurred increasingly among people who could only communicate at a distance.

This book about the Internet also benefitted greatly from the Internet. We have in mind not the software or hardware of the Internet but the people who spend time communicating online. In writing this book, we have benefitted from the thousands of contributors to the Dispute-res listserv that we have managed for the last six years and from the numerous online contacts we have made through the Center for Information Technology and Dispute Resolution and the Online Ombuds Office during the last three years.

We have had the good fortune to work with, and learn from, many organizations and entrepreneurs during the last few years. We hope that we have helped them, but they have probably helped us even more. We have served as consultants to SquareTrade.com and are most grateful to Steve Abernethy, Ahmed Khaishgi, Lalitha Vaidyanathan, Cara Cherry Lisco, and Karen Hagewood: a group of extraordinarily nice and talented people who allowed us to observe the successes and challenges of a novel "dot com" venture. We are also grateful to Karim Benyekhlef of eResolution, John Helie of Mediate.com, Colin Rule of OnlineResolution, Ernie Thiessen of SmartSettle, and the staff of the Internet Corporation for Assigned Names and Numbers (ICANN), all of whom have allowed us to see many things that we believe have enhanced our ability to write this book. We also had the benefit of working with Mark Eckstein, perhaps the world's most experienced online mediator, who handled all the mediations in our eBay pilot project and has been an ongoing resource for us.

A special thanks to David R. Johnson, an attorney with the firm of Wilmer, Cutler and Pickering in Washington, DC. We know of no one who is as creative a thinker about issues related to law and cyberspace, and almost ten years of conversations on how the online environment is influencing legal processes, approaches, and ideas are reflected on many pages of this book.

Introduction

In early 1999, we were asked by the online auction site eBay to mediate disputes that arose out of transactions between bidders and sellers. eBay was, and is, one of the most successful of online businesses. On any day at the beginning of 1999, this site had over 1.7 million items for sale. Each week there were close to a million transactions. We did not know how many disputes we would encounter, but we decided to do a two-week pilot project to judge both demand and our ability to respond.

In the middle of March 1999, eBay placed a link to our project, the Online Ombuds Office (OOO) at the University of Massachusetts, on the eBay customer service page. Even though the customer service page was three levels down from the main eBay home page, and even though no announcement about the service was made to eBay users, over one hundred and fifty complaints were filed during the following two-week period. The value of the disputes ranged from one dollar to fifteen thousand dollars. Our online mediator was able to obtain participation from both parties in more than three-quarters of the disputes and successfully mediated about

1

half. This was probably a lower success rate than would have been obtained in a traditional setting, but as a first large-scale effort, we were both satisfied and encouraged.[1]

For us, the eBay project was a turning point in an effort that had begun three years earlier.[2] We had established the Online Ombuds Office in May 1996 because we believed that, as the Internet grew, there would be a growing need for dispute resolution services. We also believed that dispute resolution services could be delivered over the Internet. We expected, in other words, that the Internet would eventually need to confront the issue of dispute resolution and that when it did, there would be opportunities to deal with the online problem using online means.

This book is about the growing world of online dispute resolution (ODR). As we will explain below, ODR draws its main themes and concepts from alternative dispute resolution (ADR) processes such as negotiation, mediation, and arbitration. ODR uses the opportunities provided by the Internet not only to employ these processes in the online environment but also to enhance these processes when they are used to resolve conflicts in offline environments. ODR is a developing field that will change as new online tools and resources are developed. Like ADR, however, at its core is the idea of providing dispute resolution in a more flexible and efficient manner than is typical with courts and litigation.

Dispute resolution is only one of many traditional societal institutions and processes that are migrating from the offline physical environment to the online virtual environment. To operate as an online entity rather than as a physical entity allows one to have a presence anywhere and to deliver a product at any time. Any informational service that can be provided faster than before, cheaper than before, and more efficiently than before, is likely to grow in demand and value, as well. For many traditional firms and institutions, therefore, the move to cyberspace has actually become more like a race than a comfortable journey.

The emergence of ODR, for reasons that we shall explain in more detail later, should be welcomed by anyone involved with or interested in opportunities to repair and improve relationships and to settle transactional disputes. Yet, any new technology can also be disruptive, particularly to those most comfortable with the old technology and with the models, approaches, and concepts that are somehow linked to that technology. For example, we believe that the overall field of dispute resolution cannot avoid being affected by the new information technologies because communication is central to this process. Change may not come as quickly in this arena as it has come, for example, to the financial community, but ODR as either a totally new approach or as a powerful add-on to traditional approaches, is something that will be harder and harder to ignore.

The Need for Online Dispute Resolution (ODR)

Our initial interest in ODR grew out of our own experiences online. We are sensitive to environments in which conflict occurs, and we routinely look in new environments to see what steps have been taken to prevent conflict and to deal with disputes. Our belief that cyberspace would not be a harmonious place was based on a very simple observation. Cyberspace seemed to us to be too active, too entrepreneurial, too competitive, and too lucrative a place for it not to have many conflicts. Even in 1996 it was apparent that cyberspace involved too many people applying their creative energies and imaginations in new ways for there not to be a need for processes to settle disputes. Cyberspace was a place where the number of transactions could only grow, and we thought, where transactions and relationships go, disputes will follow.

Our assumption that the Internet might become a kind of "dispute resolution space" and serve as a vehicle for resolving disputes was also based on a rather simple observation. This was that cyberspace was a place where powerful tools were being developed for communicating, storing, and processing information. We knew that these activities were also at the heart of dispute resolution. As capabilities for working with information and managing information online improved, we thought that opportunities for directing these capabilities at dispute resolution would also improve.

ODR and the Online Environment

Our project with eBay confirmed for us that there would be a need for ODR at active online marketplaces. It also reinforced our belief that many interesting opportunities were likely to arise for those interested in the design and application of new approaches and systems for dispute resolution. In the year and a half since completing the eBay project, our belief that ODR will have an important future has only grown. Not only has interest in our own work increased but there have been a range of developments suggesting that the emergence of ODR is likely to occur much more quickly than we had thought. For example:

- *Extraordinarily rapid growth of online commerce and online transactions.* A year and a half after we did our project with eBay, the number of items offered for sale there had increased from 1,700,000 to more than 5,000,000 and the number of transactions per week had increased to over 2,000,000.

- *Continued rapid growth of nontraditional marketplaces.* E-commerce has not grown merely by replicating offline patterns of commerce, and disputes are more likely to occur in new environments where established practices, understandings, and behaviors have not solidified. The online auction sector of the cyberspace economy is predicted to grow from three billion dollars today to twelve billion dollars in 2004.

- *More concern by governmental agencies and international bodies over problems with online transactions and more frequent advocacy of ODR as a solution.* During 2000, conferences and workshops devoted to ODR were held by the Federal Trade Commission, the Department of Commerce, the European Union, the Hague Conference on Private International Law, the Organization for Economic Cooperation and Development, the Global Business Dialogue, and the World Intellectual Property Organization.

- *Heightened interest by traditional alternative dispute resolution organizations.* Sessions on ODR were held at the annual meetings of the American Bar Association Section on Dispute Resolution, the CPR Institute of Dispute Resolution, and the Society of Professionals in Dispute Resolution (SPIDR). Significant contributions have been made by the Better Business Bureau though its BBBOnLine projects, and active ODR efforts are beginning to be undertaken by the American Arbitration Association.

- *Significant venture and private financing of online dispute resolution companies such as SquareTrade, eResolution, Cybersettle, and ClicknSettle.*

- *Evidence of being able to conduct ODR on a large scale.* The ICANN online arbitration process for domain name disputes has handled approximately two thousand complaints,[3] and SquareTrade mediated over 30,000 disputes between March and December 2000.

- *Greater acceptance by online and offline marketplaces of ODR both in settling disputes and as a mechanism for building trust.* In addition to eBay, there is a growing list of new ventures such as eLance, Onvia, HelloBrain, and others with distinctive dot com names, that offer dispute resolution to their users.

These developments have led us to believe that ODR will have even broader implications and faster growth than we originally thought it would have. It is clear that ODR has become an industry as well as a process. For E-commerce entrepreneurs, ODR is attractive as something that can be incorporated into their new ventures as part of an overall strategy to build trust among users. For online disputes, there may be no alternative to ODR, and the process may grow fastest in that context. For ODR providers, however, the ability to deliver expertise over a network becomes an asset that can be employed for disputes occurring both in and out of cyberspace. Over time, what is learned online will be applied wherever it can be of value. This is something we have already begun to see occurring in a variety of offline disputing contexts.

We have written this book to explore what ODR is and what it has the potential to become. In 1995, someone we knew who worked in the computer field told us that he thought the World Wide Web was a passing fad. We suggested to him that the Web seemed to be a system that could only expand and become ever more popular, and that we thought it would find greater and greater acceptance. Even then, we pointed out, one could, sitting at one's computer, obtain textual materials that previously required a trip to the library. He was not persuaded. There were, he said, a lot of impressive things about the Web, but who could know what would be permanent and what not?

As we write this five years later, the future existence of the Web seems completely secure. ODR, as imperfect as it may be today, also seems destined to be part of the Web's future. An active and growing Web needs ODR. The Web as a commercial space certainly needs ODR, but the Web already touches much more than commerce. Its role in education, law, politics, and other facets of our culture is growing, and these online activities will benefit from the existence of accessible online civic spaces or institutions. ODR has the potential to be one of the most important of these.

ODR and the Offline Environment

Two days before we sent this manuscript to the publisher, one of us returned home from a trip and found that the airline had lost his luggage. This seemed to be as clear a physical world event as one could imagine. Or was it? Certainly, the luggage was physical and it was sitting in some physical place somewhere. But the solutions were also, on several levels, electronic. Hope for finding the luggage lay not with the airline personnel, but with the bar code on the luggage tag and in scanning devices that might have kept track of where it had been sent. In addition, the anger and frustration that was felt was allayed somewhat when he was told that he could track the progress of the search on the Web. Instead of waiting twenty-four hours and then calling and being told whether it was found or not, he could go to a Web site and check every so often whether or not it had been found, where it might be, and when it might arrive.

This was not a problem that originated on the Web, and if it turned out that the luggage could not be found, there was no provision for filing a complaint or settling the dispute online. Yet, it also seemed quite clear that technology was moving into the world of a fairly common offline problem. It was moving a step at a time, but all that was needed for ODR was one or two more steps. Why couldn't lost luggage disputes be resolved online with a quick filing, review, and settlement of a claim? Would this not be more efficient than whatever process is normally used?

We have enough experience with cyberspace to know that what happens online inevitably touches what occurs offline. The growth in electronic commerce, for example, has caused changes in the thinking and practices of retailers whose histories were in selling offline. Similarly, the dispute resolution technologies and processes that may be originating online can be expected to manifest themselves in offline processes and institutions. Several companies, for example, have already identified ways in which Internet-based efficiencies can be applied to insurance claims that have not been handled efficiently in the past. This is only one of many possible uses offline of what exists online. Part of our goal in this book is to explain how tools and resources available over the Internet can be included in the approaches and strategies applied in offline arenas.

We are fortunate to have been participants in early experiments like the Virtual Magistrate and Online Ombuds Office projects, in the large-scale arbitration process currently being used to resolve domain name disputes, and in more recent entrepreneurial and commercially-oriented efforts like SquareTrade. We have been able to observe interest in ODR grow from only a very few individuals to an increasingly large group. In 1997, a grant from the Hewlett Foundation enabled us to establish a Center for Information Technology and Dispute Resolution at the University of Massachusetts.[4] One of our Center's principal activities, presentation of an annual

ADR Cyberweek,[5] has grown to involve approximately one thousand persons from many different countries.

Online resources will undoubtedly be part of the future of dispute resolution activity. Exactly how ODR will work, when it will be used, and what skills will be required, is less clear. The flavor of ODR employed for online disputes, for example, will frequently be different from the versions used for offline disputes. Although demand for ODR is increasing and skepticism is decreasing, many challenging questions do remain. Discussion of the issues raised by these questions forms much of the content of this book.

The Nature of ODR

Mediation and arbitration involve a range of processes that allow a neutral third party to work with parties in a dispute. A large part of the expertise of any third party consists of information management. In arbitration, there is a fairly clear process of receiving information, evaluating information, and reaching a judgment. In mediation, the process is more flexible, but decisions about which party to meet with first, what to say to each party, and how to frame and reframe information provided to each party, all involve attempts to manage the flow of information.

ODR borrows a framework from the existing models and applies technical resources and expertise that, over the Internet, can be delivered from afar. When parties are at a distance or when the need is for a cheaper and faster process than can be provided by a court, the whole process may take place online. For other disputes the use of ODR will be selective, in general being used by the third party when adding technology seems likely to improve the process in some way.

Traditional mediation is fortunate to have as its most basic feature, the face-to-face meeting, which is probably the richest of all communications encounters. During such meetings, a wink can be more meaningful than a word, and something said in a soft voice may mean something very different from the same words spoken in a loud voice. In terms of communication, therefore, it is an extremely rich, flexible, and interactive environment.

Consequently, the single question we are asked most often about ODR concerns how dispute resolution can possibly succeed without face-to-face encounters. The easiest response to this is that there are many disputes where face-to-face meetings are not feasible, and in these cases, without ODR there would be no dispute resolution process at all. ODR, we indicate, is not meant to replace or be a substitute for face-to-face settings when they can be part of the process. For online disputes, therefore, where parties may be located at great distances from each other, it is not hard to persuade even skeptics that ODR is useful and appropriate.

Although the argument that ODR can be employed when face-to-face meetings are not possible is accepted without much resistance, it may, we confess, turn out to be a bit too facile an answer. We do not think that ODR can or should replace face-to-face meetings, but as ODR grows, we do believe that it will affect the overall process of which face-to-face meetings are a part. ODR may not *replace* face-to-face meetings but it may *displace* them in the sense that the perceived need for them may change, the frequency with which they are held may change, and how they are conducted may change.

ODR, when used in offline disputes, may not yet appear to be a competitor or substitute for the face-to-face encounter. We are, quite clearly, far from being able to provide as flexible and interactive a communications process online as a meeting in a physical place. We are also not at a point where we can anticipate how videoconferencing might be employed and when it will be widely and reliably available. Where the value of ODR is likely to be recognized first in offline contexts, is at points in the process of negotiation, mediation, or arbitration that occur before or after a face-to-face meeting. While we recognize that face-to-face encounters are information-rich experiences, we also believe that what happens in between such meetings is, in terms of communication, impoverished and information-poor. What we do not see noticed by the very same people who point out to us to the great value of face-to-face encounters, is that the communications environment in which ADR is pursued *between* face-to-face meetings is often not even considered to be a period of time in which progress toward resolution is anticipated. Online tools can change this.

The Theory of ODR

ODR is dispute resolution that takes advantage of the Internet, a resource that extends what we can do, where we can do it, and when we can do it. The attraction of cyberspace can almost always be reduced to one or more of the following:

1. When one is online, one can engage in activities at a distance that previously required physical presence.

2. When one is online, one can do things quickly, if not instantaneously, that might have been inconvenient or not doable at all previously.

3. When one is online, one can acquire information processing capabilities that move beyond human capabilities in some way.

The Internet is already employed, almost routinely, for accessing information anywhere it might be located. Indeed, where something is located in a physical sense is often not a question of concern as one seeks information online. There is a wealth of information about dispute resolution that is available on the Internet from Mediate.com, CRINFO.org, ADRworld.com, and others. ODR is part of a set of developments that is going beyond merely the search for information by trying to set up processes online.

The movement from simply accessing information to participating in a process represents a maturing of the Internet. A process can be viewed as a series of informational exchanges. What makes online processes efficient is when these informational exchanges occur between human and machine, rather than between human and human. What makes the design of online processes difficult is that the range of requests permitted to the human by the system must be flexible and broad enough to satisfy the needs of the human. At the same time, however, any possible request must be anticipated so that a suitable and appropriate array of responses is programmed into the machine.

Mediation is a process in which there are large numbers of exchanges of information. It is a more complicated set of interactions than an auction, or a stock trade, or a book purchase, which is one reason we have online versions of these processes but less advanced ODR systems. As with everything else connected to computers, what appears first with ODR will be a primitive version of what will appear later. What we can be confident of, however, is that if demand exists, many familiar systems and processes that exist offline can be transformed into online systems and processes. What is understood by ODR entrepreneurs is that there is no reason why dispute resolution processes, or at least parts of them, cannot exist in electronic form and be delivered over a network.

We may not yet be able to deliver all the expertise of a mediator over a network. What we should understand, however, is that while network-delivered expertise may have limits, at least in the near future, the computer linked to the network also adds a quite novel capability: processing expertise. The network allows delivery, but what is delivered can originate with a human, with a machine, or both.

The Practice of ODR

An online dispute resolution process will be not be something that appears fully grown on a single date but rather something that evolves; not only in the capabilities that are built into it, not only in our use of it, but in how we think about it. Nothing on the Net, nor the Net itself, should be considered to be like a painting, a work of art, or even a book, that is only revealed to the public when it is completed and final. Rather, online programs and capabilities are all works in progress: usable and functional, but not final or perfected. Whether the technological object is an online auction or a dispute resolution process, there is a certain threshold of achievement that a first implementation needs to meet before it is presented to the public. However, each such technological achievement should also be judged on the basis of what it suggests about future developmental possibilities.

What will the initial incarnations of ODR be likely to include? Where will they likely be used, and what skills will they likely require of users? We shall discuss these issues in greater detail later, but looking briefly at the following three aspects of disputes should provide a framework for understanding why some dispute resolution capabilities and systems have already appeared and why we shall have to wait a bit longer for others.

Single issue versus multi-issue disputes—We already have fairly easy to use software to aid in reaching agreement when the parties disagree about only one issue, for example, money. A much greater challenge is to provide technical resources to assist parties who have many differences and where resolution depends upon identifying interests, assigning priorities, and making compromises.

Single transaction versus relationship—eBay disputes involved a single transaction with little likelihood of a future relationship. There are often several different issues that need to be dealt with in auction-related disputes, but any agreement reached is executed almost immediately. Indeed, in our eBay mediation project we felt no need even to have written agreements because there was no need for a process to monitor future performance.

Arbitration versus mediation—We already have a system in place in which thousands of disputes involving domain names and claims of trademark infringement are being arbitrated online.[6] SquareTrade[7] and others are putting

Web-based mediation systems in place, but mediation systems involve more complex interactions and require more investment than online arbitration systems.

The existence already of online systems for disputes where money is the only issue, or where there is no relationship in question, or where the dispute is arbitrated rather than mediated, is traceable to the nature of the communications process that is needed to handle such disputes. Successful online examples of the above exist because the communications infrastructure that is needed for them is at the less complex end of the spectrum. Some single transaction problems, for example, might even be handled using email, a form of software that is familiar to almost everyone with an Internet connection. Multi-issue disputes will require something more.

ClicknSettle[8] or Cybersettle[9] type "blind bidding" software, which is used for disputes where money is the only variable, requires less expertise and cost to develop than software to deal with a multi-issue dispute. With low costs of entry, it is not surprising that Cybersettle already has many competitors offering fairly similar services. Arbitration software requires a greater investment but much less of an investment than applications like those employed by SquareTrade that are focused on mediation.

The Role of Software

As we move from less complex communication to more complex communication, we move from software that might be bought "off the shelf," in that it is ubiquitous and requires minimal online skills, to software that does more but requires more. We shall discuss this in greater detail later, but if there is anything that is central to the capabilities we have for interacting online, both for delivering expertise and enhancing expertise, it is software. A principal challenge for anyone or any group wishing to provide dispute resolution services over the Net is to find or design software that handles sophisticated levels of communication and yet does not have a high learning curve for users. This is a considerable challenge because if the third party or even one of the disputants is unable to use the software effectively, the process will not work optimally.

The acceptance and development of ODR will accelerate as the general level of comfort and sophistication in using online tools increases. For parties to participate equally requires that the software employed not frustrate them. Indeed, while third parties are commonly concerned with the relative power of disputants, sensitivity to how the online environment affects power relationships is one of the lessons third parties will need to learn.

How This Book Works

We begin the book by identifying the novel and powerful characteristics of the electronic environment that open up the possibilities for ODR. Disputes and dispute resolution do not occur in a vacuum, and Chapter One provides the framework for anyone interested in working with ODR. The setting and context in which any dispute arises will provide us not only with information about the nature of the dispute but also about the options that might be considered in trying to resolve it.

Chapter Two looks at activities during the last ten years that have involved ODR. The idea of ODR has been "in the air" for a few years and there have been several noteworthy experiments. The recent history of online dispute resolution activities can probably be divided into three time periods. The first, from 1990–1995, involved largely informal efforts to resolve disputes generally linked to university-based environments. The second, from 1995–1998, involved several foundation and university-connected projects that were open to all and were intended to assist users with disputes involving intellectual property or involving Internet Service Providers. They were begun largely by lawyers who were involved in cyberlaw activities of various kinds. Since 1999, there has been much greater activity, mostly entrepreneurial in nature, and often more focused on particular dispute arenas than earlier projects were. The era of 1999 to the present coincides with and is related to the growth in electronic commerce. We conclude the chapter by taking a peek at some emerging trends and developments.

Chapter Three looks at the basic goals and qualities of any ODR system. We suggest that every successful ODR system can be looked at as a triangle with one side representing access, convenience, and ease of use, a second side representing trust in the fairness of the process, and the third side representing the degree of expertise being delivered to users. These three elements must be present at some threshold level in any valid ODR process. Different systems may provide different measures of the three factors, and the strengths and weaknesses of the system will be visible in the resulting shape of the triangle.

Chapter Four examines the beginning of the ODR process and introduces the concept of the "fourth party." We suggest that the role of technology can be understood by considering it to be a kind of "fourth party," working with and assisting the traditional third party. In looking at the processes of complaining online and the subsequent process of engaging the respondent, the concept of the "fourth party" can be employed to understand various differences with offline processes.

Chapter Five focuses on the use of the network as a supplement to dispute resolution that occurs mainly offline. We are confident that there will be an increased blending of ADR and ODR. Here, too, thinking of technology and the network in terms of a "fourth party" is a useful way to understand the contribution that can be made by including online resources in the resolution of offline disputes.

Chapter Six explores the role of the "fourth party" when ODR is exclusively online. This will occur mainly in disputes arising out of online activities and when the parties are located at distant locations. In thinking about ODR and comparing it with ADR, we suggest that ODR, when used exclusively, becomes a "screen-to-screen" process. If ODR is to be successful it must place information on the screen in a manner that enhances communication and allows it to occur in ways that may not be present in face-to-face interactions.

We conclude Chapter Six by looking at the ODR practitioner. Just as the online environment is bringing changes to those who practice law, sell stocks, or run for office, it will affect those who are concerned with dispute resolution. There are not only issues of skills and competencies but concerns about ethical standards that need to be addressed. There are challenges for the dispute resolution community and also opportunities. We hope that this book contributes to overcoming the challenges and building upon the opportunities.

1

The Impact of Cyberspace on Disputes and Dispute Resolution

The Demand for ODR, *What ODR Offers;* **ADR and ODR,** *The Limits of Litigation in the Information Age, Behind the Growth of ODR;* **Virtual Places and Virtual Processes,** *What Is a Virtual Space? Describing and Understanding Virtual Spaces, Online Tools and Online Spaces;* **Current Types of Online Spaces,** *Online Auctions, Online Banks;* **Building a Dispute Resolution Space,** *Where Should Dispute Resolution Spaces Be?; Basic Building Choices, Enhancing ODR Space.*

One morning in late 1998, we received a letter from a lawyer in Los Angeles threatening to sue us for trademark violation. It seems that we had recently registered the domain name "cyberjustice.org" without first checking to see whether the word "cyberjustice" had been trademarked. The lawyer said that he had trademarked the word and that under trademark law he owned it. He said that for us to use the domain name would infringe upon his trademark. He demanded that we transfer the domain name to him, and if we did not do that and do it quickly, he would file suit.

Although we had been involved in our share of disputes, this was actually the first time either of us had been threatened with litigation. What was particularly surprising to us was that of all the possible kinds of lawsuits that we might have been threatened with, we were involved in a trademark dispute. Trademarks were the business of corporations like CocaCola or IBM. Domain names aside, if we had wanted to violate a trademark, it would have been difficult to think of a way to do it.

Among other things, the letter caused us to think of all the new activities that the Internet makes possible that were not possible before. We can form relationships with people in faraway places and we can transact business with anyone anywhere. In the pre-Internet world we would not have had the opportunity to violate trademark law, but the Internet empowers us to do all kinds of novel things. Getting into disputes in new ways is one of them.

We had registered the "cyberjustice" domain name with the thought that we might use it for ODR activities. It certainly seemed ironic that the word had brought us into a dispute rather than helping us to resolve disputes. We thought, however, that we should suggest to this lawyer that we employ ODR to resolve the problem and, at least, we might gain some ODR experience. Unfortunately, the lawyer had no interest in anything short of total victory. By this time, as well, we had realized that his claims about our violating his trademark were not as clear as he had made them out to be. For example, there was no reason for him to think that our activities would be confused with his, which is one of the key issues in trademark law. Finally and fortunately, we stopped hearing from him.

We were sorry that our offer to try to resolve this dispute online was not accepted. We had mediated a variety of domain name disputes and had usually found that acceptable solutions in domain name disputes were possible. We still believe that because cyberspace is such a large and expandable place, a place where there should be no real need to compete for space, creative mediation can lead to interesting win-win, or at least sharing, opportunities. This is not, unfortunately, an argument that most trademark holders are willing to accept. We shall discuss later the ODR system that is currently being used, and being used quite often, to arbitrate domain name disputes. Our dispute occurred before this system had been put in place, and we felt fortunate that we did not end up in court.

The system for arbitrating some domain name and trademark disputes emerged because there were a great number of such disputes and there was pressure for a dispute resolution process that was quicker and less expensive than litigation. During 2000, online mediation systems were also set up to deal with consumer-related E-commerce disputes—another arena in which disputes are plentiful. It is not surprising that ODR is emerging most rapidly in such environments. As the value of ODR is proven in these arenas, however, we believe that the demand for broader-based dispute resolution systems will grow. ODR is part of the movement to build civic institutions online, and these institutions and systems are greatly needed to encourage online activity and growth.

ODR is not totally new. In the next chapter, we shall discuss a variety of experiments and projects that have occurred over the last ten years. What has changed recently is the level of entrepreneurial activity and the demand for high-quality online tools and resources that could be employed in ODR. ODR is a response to the disputes and other activities that are appearing online, and it is also a user of resources becoming available in cyberspace. Its nature, therefore, will reflect various qualities and features of the online environment.

ODR is also not totally new in a second way. ODR has roots in the ADR movement that has been growing for the last twenty-five years. ODR has qualities acquired from the online environment, but it also has traits acquired from ADR. This chapter explores the nature of this new organism, and how the novel qualities of the Internet are shaping its emerging form. More particularly, this chapter discusses three key issues.

1. Where is the demand for ODR coming from and why is demand accelerating?

2. What existing resources, models, approaches, and people with appropriate expertise can this new civic institution build upon?

3. What can we build online and what should we build?

The Demand for ODR

In his 1989 book *The Cuckoo's Egg*, Clifford Stoll described the detective work that was needed to track down a seventy-five cent accounting discrepancy in the computer account at Lawrence Livermore Laboratory. Stoll quickly discovered that a hacker had broken into the system and had used a little time that could not be billed to any existing user. Stoll then approached the local FBI office and asked them to try to find the hacker.

The FBI refused Stoll's request, indeed laughed at it, because all they could see was a possible crime involving seventy-five cents. They told Stoll that if he encountered a crime involving a million dollars, they might become interested.

Since that time, the Federal government has built a significant infrastructure to deal with online crime. It has recognized that to be successful it needs online tools and resources and relationships with counterparts in other countries. Breaking into computer systems is now understood to be as serious, and often more serious, than breaking into a physical structure. This is not a book about online crime, but there are some clear lessons that can be learned from the more than decade-long experience with cybercrime. We know, for example, that the range and variety of interactions at a distance is probably much greater than we would have thought, that they are of greater value than we might have imagined, and that disruptions in service can be very costly. Many of us are more dependent on our Internet connection than we would have predicted. It is still not possible to physically assault someone online—although we shall recount the story of a "virtual rape in cyberspace" in the next chapter—but the opportunities for creating and being involved in many different kinds of online conflict are growing.

Using the Internet, we have devised new ways to create value and new ways to cause problems. Stoll's hacker turned out to be located in Germany. Stoll gradually learned that not only did he have a problem getting the attention of the FBI in this country, but that once he did, the "arm of the law" lost most of its strength when it tried to cross a national border. The law has a very large set of rules to answer jurisdictional questions, but even these rules do not cover every problem arising out of cross-border transactions. ODR largely ignores jurisdictional questions, relying instead on the desire of the parties to resolve a problem out of court. Consequently, demand for ODR grows every time the issue of jurisdiction surfaces.

One of the technological facts in Stoll's book that is easy to skip is that the hacker was connecting to the Internet at 1200 bytes per second. Many of us now connect one hundred times faster than that. The screen that the hacker was looking at in Germany probably had green or white letters on a black background, with no variation in font size and no images as we have today. The hacker was not clicking on links or spending time surfing the Web for the simple reason that there was no World Wide Web in 1986.

Changes in all these aspects of computing are important because how fast one communicates affects how much interaction is possible. It affects how many cycles of interaction can occur in a particular period of time. When we learn to employ images and communicate graphically, our expressive capabilities further expand. We can do more both in terms of time and in terms of range of expression, and get feedback from others faster. We could not have had an efficient ODR process in 1986 with the equipment available then, but we also, except for the occasional hacker or two, would not expect many disputes either.

One thing was understood in 1986 that is still of central importance; text, images, pictures, and sounds can all be stored and communicated as strings of zeroes and ones. Information that formerly was transmitted in some kind of physical format can now be stored, organized, and communicated in electronic form. To paraphrase Nicholas Negroponte, we can now transmit bits when before we had to transport atoms.[1]

What ODR Offers

Marshall McLuhan once wisely wrote that when "a new technology comes into a social milieu it cannot cease to permeate that milieu until every institution is saturated."[2] What McLuhan wisely did not predict was how fast this would occur. The rate of change is affected by both technology and culture. With a fast network and powerful machines connected to the network, there are opportunities for doing new things in new ways. The possible market for anything I might wish to sell includes anyone who is online. When my product is composed of bits, which is almost anything that has to do with information, I can create it faster and deliver it faster.

While all this is true, technological advances alone are rarely enough to change old institutions and practices. People must also be ready, able, and willing to use the technology. As we shall examine in detail in Chapter Three, powerful systems will not bring change if they are not used, and they will not be used if they are too difficult to use or are not trusted. Those arenas in which incentives to make use of ODR are highest and resistance is lowest will likely be in the first wave of ODR applications. Therefore, the attention given to ODR in the consumer arena and its growing use there is not surprising. Consider the following:

- *Tools*—The tools employed for relatively simple transactional disputes need not be as sophisticated as the online resources that will be required for more complex transactions or disputes involving ongoing relationships. More powerful tools generally require more training and this will deter some participants.

- *Skills*—By the mere fact that they have purchased or sold something online, the parties to a consumer dispute are likely to have a higher than average comfort level with the online environment. In general, they are more likely to be able to use Web-based tools and not be limited only to email. Again, more powerful tools will require a higher level of skills from all participants. As we shall discuss later, interactions among the participants will occur at the skill level of the least skillful, not the most skillful.

- *Acknowledgment of disputes*—While businesses often have customer service departments, they are also often reluctant to

acknowledge that their transactions lead to disputes.
Having an ODR service at an online marketplace constitutes
an admission that there are disputes and, perhaps, an
admission that disputes are at such a level that action needs to
be taken. This concern about what ODR might signify to
users surprised us at first since we encountered it even in
marketplaces in which everyone was quite aware that there
were disputes. Yet, it was still a commonly held belief that if
one competitor admitted that disputes occurred and the other
did not, the first might be perceived less positively and be at a
competitive disadvantage.

Offering ODR at a marketplace should be seen as positive,
as adding value to the marketplace, and as something that
provides a competitive advantage. We think that the presence
of an ODR provider at a marketplace should attract new users
and increase willingness to participate in transactions. As
market leaders such as eBay insert dispute resolution as a basic
feature of their sites, we would expect the positives of an ODR
presence to be more widely recognized.

In many online marketplaces, such as those involving
auctions or barter, the marketplace owner is not a party to
disputes that occur there and may be more willing to admit
that all transactions may not go smoothly. Perhaps more
importantly, many small businesses that are selling in such
marketplaces do not have customer service departments and
have little experience dealing with dissatisfied customers. As a
consequence, online businesses need to find ways to assure
people that their service is reliable and trustworthy. In
particular, they need the kind of seals or trustmarks offered by
BBBOnLine, TrustE, SquareTrade, or WebAssured to indicate
that the seller has met the standards imposed by these groups
in order to acquire a seal.

- Cost—For ODR, like any new service, it takes some period of
  time for the marketplace to determine its value. If its value to
  a marketplace is high, the marketplace may be willing to

subsidize an ODR process and consider it one more service being provided to users. If the value of the item in dispute is high but the transaction is not complex, parties may find it in their interest to pay for the service since the cost may be relatively low. Over time, the use of technology should also make intervention in some common disputes less costly. Currently, SquareTrade offers its "Direct Negotiation" process for free but charges when a mediator gets involved.

The "Direct Negotiation" process, which we shall examine in more detail later, allows disputants to communicate with each other through SquareTrade's software. The success rate is close to 80 percent, a rather astonishing percentage. When this fails, parties pay a fee for a human mediator to work with the parties. What is clear from the SquareTrade experience and what had never been achieved before, is that consumers will pay for ODR. How much particular disputes should cost and how much mediators and arbitrators with online skills might be able to charge has not yet been determined. We strongly believe that parties to disputes, even offline disputes, will expect third parties to have online skills and will see less value in third parties who are not as comfortable online as the parties themselves.

In the next section, we shall discuss the relationship between ODR and ADR. While we are often asked how dispute resolution can occur without face-to-face sessions, over time the question may be how one can resolve disputes without use of technology. ODR does borrow from ADR, but in the future, ADR will also borrow from ODR.

ADR and ODR

One of us, Janet, has focused her career on the area of dispute resolution. The other one of us, Ethan, has worked mainly in the area of law and technology. Our interest in ODR arose from trying to see whether there were points of intersection between technology and

ADR and, if so, what kinds of sparks might result from their coming together?

We understood that technology is often employed to create new tools and we also understood that technology is employed to create new environments in which the tools can be used. As we looked at ADR, we wondered whether any of the new tools would be of value in ADR and whether ADR would be of value in the new environments that were being created. We knew alternative dispute resolution had started out as an alternative to litigation but had become the primary means for dispute resolution. Would the new information technologies create an alternative to the alternative or would it simply change the alternative and, if so, what kind of change was likely?

There is no mystery to the recent popularity of ADR. Compared to litigation, ADR has the following advantages:

- Lower cost
- Greater speed
- More flexibility in outcomes
- Less adversarial
- More informal
- Solution rather than blame-oriented
- Private
- Fewer jurisdictional problems

We still employ trials, and even encourage them, when the goal is to protect someone's rights, clarify a point of law, or set a standard for public behavior. Sometimes plaintiffs want to go to trial when the outcome they seek is a finding in which one party wins and the other loses. In addition, if revenge or destroying the other party is a goal, courts and trials will continue to be attractive.

ADR has grown because rights and revenge are not the focus of most disputes. Many disputes involve misunderstandings, accidents, or other situations where getting the problem resolved quickly is more important than placing blame. Disputes may involve parties who might see some possibility of working together in the future, and removing hostility might even be more valuable than getting compensation. Frequently, getting something resolved quickly is important because taking too much time will cost more than the value of whatever is involved in the dispute. In the Internet environment and in information-related industries, these factors are likely to be even more important. Where the value of information declines quickly over time, litigation becomes an even less desirable option. The dispute described in the case of *Whelan v. Jaslow* discussed in the next section is a good illustration of the limits of litigation in this context.

ADR moved dispute resolution "out of court." ODR moves it even further away from court. The paradigm of dispute resolution had traditionally been the trial, a process that only took place in a physical place: a courtroom. Part of the attraction of ADR was that it moved dispute resolution out of the courtroom and courthouse, moving it from an identifiable place to any place. Courts today are eager to send cases to mediation and arbitration, but twenty-five years ago, the idea of moving dispute resolution "out of court" encountered concern similar to the concern expressed today about moving dispute resolution to the arena of cyberspace.

The trend toward nonlegalistic systems of settling conflict is likely to continue, pushing mediation and arbitration more clearly into the foreground and litigation further into the background. Looked at in a different way, the growth of ADR represented a move away from a fixed place and also away from a fixed and formal process. As this has occurred, we have become increasingly comfortable with dispute resolution taking place anywhere, whether in a school, factory, store, or office. ODR, by designating cyberspace as a location for dispute resolution, is, we believe, simply extending this trend further, moving the process not only from some mutually agreed-upon physical place but to a virtual place. As we discuss the nature of "virtual places" below, we shall see how feasible it is to accomplish this.

The emergence of ODR is closely linked to the appearance of powerful networking capabilities, but it is the broad acceptance of alternatives to litigation and the idea that justice can be applied anywhere, that might be considered the beginning of the road to ODR. Over the last quarter century, ADR has proven that moving justice away from the courthouse is often desirable and that the arena of dispute resolution, once thought to be the exclusive domain of law and courts, is markedly different from what it was several decades ago. Mediation, arbitration, and other forms of "alternative" dispute resolution are now the most common approaches to dealing with conflict. While at one time the thought of suing and "going to court" may have been the first thought of someone with a problem, we know today that "going out of court" is the route that is most likely to bring satisfaction. As an example of how hiring lawyers to battle in court can be more destructive than beneficial, consider the following dispute. This occurred some time ago, but it is one dispute in which winning in court may not have been the most desirable outcome.

The Limits of Litigation in the Information Age

One of the landmark cases of copyright law as it relates to software is the case of *Whelan v. Jaslow*.[3] The plaintiff, Whelan, was a computer programmer who had created software to automate the defendant's dental laboratory. The software, which ran on a minicomputer, satisfied the defendant, and the two parties began a joint venture—using Whelan's programming expertise and Jaslow's contacts in the dental service industry—to market the program, called Dentalab, to other dental laboratories. The relationship between Whelan and Jaslow was not harmonious, but the business venture was viable and survived until a significant event in the history of computing occurred: the arrival of the IBM personal computer in 1981.

The Dentalab program, which was owned by the programmer Whelan, would not run on the IBM PC, and Jaslow decided that he had learned enough so that he could conquer the PC market without Whelan. In creating a new program that would run on the PC,

Jaslow not only looked at the source code for Dentalab but modeled many of the screens and functions of the new program on Dentalab. The similarities between the two programs were so stark that the judge ruled that Whelan's rights had been infringed. She was awarded attorneys' fees and $101,000, the amount of the profits Jaslow had made from sales of his PC program.

As we have thought about this dispute over the years, we have always believed that the lost opportunity was the most important lesson in this case. Although the court clearly did rule that screen displays are protectable, it is equally clear that the business partnership was ruined and economic opportunities were lost. There is, of course, no guarantee that mediation or any dispute resolution process could have successfully restored and refocused the Whelan-Jaslow partnership or that the partnership would have conquered the turbulent 1980s software environment. Yet, no one seemed cognizant of or prepared to do anything about the fact that the value of the information at the heart of this dispute was declining rapidly as time passed.

It may be that the attorneys, and probably the parties as well, saw the Whelan-Jaslow relationship, at the time the litigation commenced, as being over and without any possibility of salvaging. Perhaps it was. Yet, mediators and other experts in dispute resolution might have had a different perspective. One difference between litigation and mediation is that mediators recognize that by maintaining lines of communication, by placing few or no limits on what issues are raised, and by placing the burden for resolution on the parties, more often than not the unanticipated occurs and the seemingly unresolvable is resolved.[4] It is of little concern that ideas for how this relationship might have been restored are difficult to imagine. Imagining reasonable outcomes is often a fruitless exercise at the beginning of a mediation. What mediators assume is that the mediation process is able to tap the creativity of the parties and elicit ideas that were hidden or appeared to be irrelevant. As a result, damaged relationships are often rebuilt or reestablished in ways that had not appeared possible at the start.

Litigation can be damaging to both parties because it can distract the parties from what they need to do in the marketplace. Mediation can strive to reduce hostility between the parties, to fashion an agreement about tasks each party is willing to assume, and to reach agreement on methods for making certain that tasks have been carried out. In *Whelan v. Jaslow*, what might have become clear in mediation was that everything they had built was losing value quickly as time passed. They had a small time window to exploit any advantage they might have had, and only by somehow creating a working relationship could that happen. Either side may have thought that they might obtain a high market share and a competitive advantage from a court decision. Yet, when technology is changing rapidly and the value of almost anything decreases rather than increases over time, standards that are announced in a judge's decision may be less significant than they would be in a slowly changing environment.

Behind the Growth of ODR

There have been two main catalysts behind ADR's growth. For some, ADR is viewed as an opportunity for better or more appropriate resolutions than can be provided in court. As the *Whelan* case illustrates, litigation tends to end with one party being the winner and the other the loser. The ideal of ADR is a win-win solution, an outcome that the parties are satisfied with and which might even allow them to work together further in the future.

The second force fueling the growth of ADR is bureaucratic. It is viewed as a means to save money and reduce court caseloads by moving disputes out of court. The largest source of referrals for mediators remains the court system. The enthusiasm of the justice system for ADR is less a concern over obtaining better or fairer solutions than it is a way to meet bureaucratic needs and to process cases faster and more cheaply than can be done at trial.

As we observe the growth of ODR, we shall also see it employed for a range of reasons. Governmental authorities support ODR because it is costly for parties who are at a distance to sue, and there can be difficult jurisdictional problems to solve, particularly in cross-border transactions. ODR certainly will also be assumed to reduce costs by avoiding the expenses of face-to-face meetings. Others will view ODR as a means to meet the needs of persons or groups who might have no other options for dispute settlement or who would not go to court even if they could. And for still others, often those involved in offline disputes, ODR will be looked to not as something that will be employed in lieu of ADR, but something that can be employed to enhance ADR.

We shall no doubt also see experiments by courts to use the Internet to expedite litigation and enhance access.[5] The legal system, however, is subject to rules and standards enforced by bar associations and others. Lawyers and the legal system are responding to the forces of technology, but as developments in dispute resolution during the last two decades indicate, much more innovation and experimentation is likely to occur outside the legal system than within it.

It is interesting to note that there are several Internet start-ups that hope to provide legal services online.[6] The motivating idea is that if lawyers have expertise and the expertise is informational in nature, it should be deliverable electronically. These ventures may ultimately be successful, but at every step of the way there are fifty state bar associations looking at them, trying to assess whether law is being practiced without a license and whether rules of legal ethics are being violated. ODR is "out of court" and out of the focused eye of the state and the profession. It is as free to design and apply the technological applications described in the next section as any other venture in E-commerce would be.

Virtual Places and Virtual Processes

A basic attraction of the Internet is the ability to do at a distance what previously required physical presence. Anyone who has used the Internet is also aware that informational exchanges and interactions can occur more quickly than before. The word "cyberspace," however, suggests that as these exchanges accelerate and multiply, what occurs is more than the accumulation or rapid transmission of a large batch of data. In addition to all this, we are gaining access to new spaces, "cyberspaces," that allow users anywhere to accomplish many tasks that might have previously occurred in physical spaces.

We have, of course, always had some capability to communicate at a distance. The spoken word can be passed on from person to person, and the development of writing thousands of years ago enabled documents to travel over space and also, when a document was preserved, to travel over time. More recently, the telephone, television, and fax machine have enabled us to accelerate communication at a distance and to interact and exchange documents in ways that were not possible from afar. What the Internet allows are many different forms of communication and interaction to be structured and organized on a Web "site" in a way that gives us something novel: virtual places and virtual processes. It is as a result of this new capability to build sophisticated online spaces and processes that we can try to consider what a virtual dispute resolution space might look like and what varieties of dispute resolution spaces we can expect to see.

What Is a Virtual Space?

The Internet is often said to reduce the importance of space and distance. This is true in the sense that communication can occur easily among persons in different places, and information can be accessed quickly from anywhere. Space and distance interfere less with the process of communication than they used to. If information is online, we can get it quickly and conveniently. And if people are online, we become closer to them.

In another sense, however, the Internet makes space more important and the use of space more complicated. The Internet allows us to create new kinds of spaces—spaces that are not physical in nature but exist online in virtual form. The Internet can be viewed as having an unlimited number of building lots, with the capabilities for building structures improving as tools and materials improve. These are spaces where we can structure interactions that we never thought of before, because time and distance factors had led us to believe that they were not possible. Some of these online spaces are already the focal point of great activity but how best to build them, design them, and use them for different kinds of services is not yet perfectly clear.

Any space, physical or virtual, is an environment where many different interactions, usually focused on one or a small set of goals, occur. A courthouse, for example, is a space oriented around law, a store is focused on business, a health club about exercise, and so forth. As noted earlier, ADR was a movement that moved dispute resolution out of the courthouse. Leaving the courthouse involved leaving a space that was formal and, for nonlawyers, was intimidating. Among the goals of ADR was to make access to justice more accessible than it might be in a courthouse, and one way of doing this was to bring the parties together wherever it was convenient. ADR was less concerned than law with the symbolism a particular place might represent. Indeed, the flexibility of ADR was emphasized when the parties and the third-party neutral met in an office, factory, schoolyard, office building, indeed anywhere.

With ODR and the creation of effective online spaces, access to justice-related processes can be increased even further. Participants can be anywhere, and entry to any virtual dispute resolution space is as easy as clicking a mouse. Where ODR does differ from ADR, however, is that while the characteristics of the space in which parties meet is not important for ADR, the nature and design of the virtual space in which ODR occurs is extraordinarily important, indeed critical. We shall describe later our suggestion that technology can be considered to be a "fourth party." Part of the influence of this "fourth party" comes from the online "space" in which ODR takes place. The nature of the online space will shape how expertise is delivered and the manner in which the parties will be able to interact. With ODR, the place *is* the process in the sense that the functions built into a site, and the appearance and arrangement of a site, will structure what is and what is not possible to occur there. Success rates can change significantly by redesigning a Web site or even changing a detail or two. An ODR site with fewer features may be quite adequate for simpler disputes, just as email alone may be adequate for many disputes. Yet, a space with broad information processing built in can enhance a third party's skills in ways that may not be possible offline. As ODR grows, we can expect to have a range of spaces developed, with those at the high end fostering a richer, and possibly also more complex, interaction among the parties. This would be a space that not only allows a mediator to exercise a range of skills but also enhances the mediator's expertise.

Describing and Understanding Virtual Spaces

Margaret Wertheim has written that "every different kind of space requires a different kind of language."[7] Our language about space is largely, and not surprisingly, related to physical settings. The labels that tend to be used to describe virtual spaces are labels that have been used in connection with physical spaces. Thus, we have online stores, online malls, online casinos, online conference centers, online auctions, and so forth. Using these labels has the effect of making them seem familiar and making us more comfortable with these sites. We use these labels because we do not yet have an adequate set of words to describe the novel qualities of these virtual spaces. Yet, these online places are not identical to their physical counterparts. In many instances, therefore, the use of familiar labels masks significant differences and misleads us into thinking that the virtual and the physical entities are identical, or that the virtual is just a copy of the physical that can be accessed anywhere and at any time.

The struggle to describe and explain how the Web is both similar to and different from physical counterparts is one that has been with us since Web sites first started to appear. Early Web sites were built by persons who discovered that colorful and informative "home pages" could be built by persons with relatively little technical skill. These home pages tended to consist of a single screen that usually had some information about the person who developed the site and a list of hyperlinks, items that a user could click on that would "take them" to some other site. One could have a site that was useful not because there was original content on it but because there were links to other sites that did have rich content. What was attractive and novel at the time, was that at low cost and with modest skills, one could provide access to all the information about a topic that existed on any Web site anywhere. Anyone, it was said, could become a publisher and "pages" were what publishers produced. Interestingly, as Web sites have become more dynamic environments with the screen looking and acting less and less like a fixed page of print, the use of the term "home page" has been declining.

Some, at that time, described the Web as being a giant library or a library without walls. The Web was, of course, an informational space just as a library is an informational space, and the library label probably helped a bit in allowing new users to understand that there was much informational content on the Web. Today, we rarely see the Web labeled as a library. The library metaphor has faded partly because the Web now contains stores, meeting places, and other nonlibrary kinds of spaces, but partly because the label was not really appropriate. Physical libraries are places that have filtered and organized information and employ librarians who add value to information. The Web, with no space limits to deal with, provided access to information anywhere, but the lack of space limits also meant that many decisions were not made because they did not have to be made. The Web had one of a library's most significant ingredients, information, but little else that a library has.

As time has passed, we have seen a variety of metaphors for cyberspace come and go. For example, cyberspace is rarely referred to any more as an "information superhighway." That metaphor focused attention on the capability for communicating information at electronic speed but ignored all other features of the online environment. We seem to have already reached the point when no single metaphor can work very well. The Internet is a multifunction space just as most physical spaces are, and what is ongoing is the building online of spaces for an enormous variety of purposes, one of which being dispute resolution. The inability to suggest what the Web is in a single word should be taken as a good sign and a sign of its growth and development. It also indicates that there are few limits to the kinds of novel spaces that can be built online.

Online Tools and Online Spaces

As we see more and more specialized ODR spaces appearing, it is easy to confuse virtual spaces with virtual tools. Before you begin to think through how you might want to utilize ODR in your work, it is important for you to distinguish between these two. Tools provide a means for doing a particular informational task or a small set of informational tasks. Every online space will have tools as a component—perhaps a large array of tools. What will give these spaces character, however, and indeed differentiate them from each other, will be a combination of the tools included, the manner in which they are presented and coordinated, and the other resources that are made available.

The relationship of specialized tools to specialized spaces has parallels in the physical office environment. Once an empty office is furnished and arranged, it will have an array of tools, and it will be organized in some fashion that is believed to further the mission of the enterprise. Just as there can be many designs for airports, arenas, shopping malls, and other physical spaces, we can expect there will be many versions of online dispute resolution spaces. Some virtual spaces may be primarily concerned with complex disputes, others with offline disputes, others with consumer disputes, and so on. As electronic tools improve, such spaces will become more powerful and perhaps more varied than physical spaces because there are no obstacles of time and space to limit designs.

The most familiar online tool is probably email. The first experience of most persons when they are introduced to the Internet typically involves email, a tool for sending messages from one place to another at electronic speed. It is an easy-to-use tool and a tool whose value is easy to see. Email has the virtue of simplicity, and for quick exchanges between people, it is a highly effective and appropriate tool. Our challenge is that no tool can be expected to handle all informational and communication tasks equally well. For ODR, we need online spaces, not simply an online tool or two. We need a range of communication and information management tools that are easy to use, powerful, and flexible. Email may certainly be one of these tools. It is a moderately flexible tool and it may be flexible and powerful enough to be employed when parties are few, exchanges are few, and issues are few. The more ambitious we wish to be, however, the more we will benefit from, for example, Web-based tools designed to organize information, allow collaboration in drafting agreements, evaluate information, foster brainstorming, monitor performance, clarify interests and priorities of the parties, and more.

Current Types of Online Spaces

We are at a stage in which we have some tools, but there are still opportunities to create more advanced tools and to create multifaceted and flexible virtual spaces where the tools can facilitate ODR. Email is so familiar that imagining other ways of interacting online may be difficult. If so, here are a few examples of online spaces that are widely used, are easy to use, and that manage and focus the flow of information and data very efficiently.

Online Auctions

Online auctions allow sellers to determine who among many bidders is willing to pay the highest price. Online auctions allow an efficient many-to-many communication pattern and, as this occurs according to the rules prescribed at the site, knowledge of who is willing to pay the highest price emerges. As with any online space where something happens and where there is a process rather than simply information that can be accessed, managing the flow of information is critical. At most online auctions, for example, communication among bidders is limited to price. Communication between any bidder and a seller, however, can involve anything.

Online auctions are not extremely complex spaces but they are not simple either. In addition to informing bidders of information items such as what the object being sold is and looks like, what the highest bid is, and how much time is left in the auction, there must be information that encourages interested bidders to actually place a bid. Sellers usually do not have recognizable brand names, and trust among participants in the auctions may not be high. Every seller therefore, must figure out how to build trust, something that is not easy when it may not be clear where someone is physically located. Building the software that announces items for sale and manages bidding, therefore, was not all that was needed before the auction sites would be used. What was added was a system for allowing bidders to check on the reputation of the seller; this feature was needed in the virtual space, while an offline auction site might not have needed to provide it. This is done through a feedback system. Here in Figure 1.1 is a typical feedback rating screen that is used by eBay.

Auction sites have attracted a wide following partly because they allow a form of interaction that cannot take place offline at the same scale. In addition, they provide mechanisms for building trust and offer informational and communication options so that parties can feel comfortable that they know what they are bidding on, can make their own assessment of its value, and can feel confident that the item will be delivered if they place the highest bid. It should be obvious that the process of online auctions would not have grown as it has if offers had to be submitted via email, viewed by a human, and parties then were notified via email.

Auction sites are relevant to ODR not only because they have been designed with the information management capabilities of the

FIGURE 1.1 Sample eBay Feedback Rating.

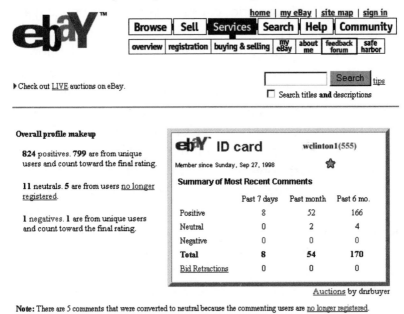

Note: There are 5 comments that were converted to neutral because the commenting users are no longer registered.

You can leave feedback for this user. Visit the Feedback Forum for more info on feedback profiles.

If you are welinton1 ( ) ⭐, you can respond to comments in this Feedback Profile.

Internet in mind, and not only because they are another example of an Internet space that was not thought of by persons in the offline auction industry, but because they can be looked at as a kind of specialized ODR site in which differences are resolved. What the auction does is foster a multiparty competition in which a winner is determined. The best auction sites not only have many items for sale but have an array of tools for locating and evaluating information, for engaging users, for building trust, and for reducing the sense of risk. The ultimate issue in an auction is price, but no one will participate if there is a lack of trust. Online auctions, even though they have an innately distrustful atmosphere, have succeeded because of software that makes the auction a convenient multiparty negotiation space and that integrates devices for building trust.

Online Banks

Virtual banking spaces are possible because, while banks may appear to most people to be financial or monetary institutions, they are actually informational institutions. Banks need to be able to maintain records and accounts, transfer data about these accounts (this is called making a payment, or withdrawing money, or depositing money), and persuade users that they can be trusted to perform these functions without error. Many of us have salary checks deposited directly in our bank accounts, not by having our employer carry a huge bundle of paper checks to the bank, but by sending electronic messages that end up moving data (money) out of the employer's account and into that of the employee.

Online banking spaces try to make users comfortable doing what they have traditionally done inside physical banks, and then add capabilities for working with their accounts. Once money is represented by bits, it can be sent or received as payments, or even sent instantaneously to an online brokerage house.

We shall discuss later how any ODR space must be convenient, trustworthy, and deliver value. For those who use online banking spaces, these conditions are satisfied. They are certainly convenient for paying bills, they deliver value by allowing you to view accounts from anywhere at any time, and they are trustworthy to the extent that there are ways to contact a physical person at the bank if needed.

The value that online banks provide in the speed with which one can pay bills or check accounts is matched by the ability to do things that cannot be done inside physical banks. Any online informational space can do anything it wants to do with the information it has. A bank's information is not information as we normally think of it, but money. As the tools present in online banking spaces are increased and enhanced, they will, as long as trust is maintained, provide value that is not available in physical banks.

Building a Dispute Resolution Space

We are interested in what dispute resolution spaces should look like, not how auction, bank, or marketplace spaces are set up. It is useful for you to think about the appearance, functions, and approaches of such sites and how they reveal the kind of thought and imagination that is needed to build any site where the challenge is to manage online information and interactions, thereby providing both convenience and trust. It is the successes and failures of these sites that can guide our thinking about what we would like to have in an ODR space, what the minimum array of features such a space should contain, and what we might hope to see added on over time.

Where Should Dispute Resolution Spaces Be?

You may think this is an odd question, since one of the most prized features of cyberspace is that a site can be accessible regardless of where it is physically located. Yet, the question of "where" does arise when we consider whether a dispute resolution space should be freestanding or connected in some way with another site.

There are many sites that are only usable by those who share some affiliation or have some other quality in common. A site, for example, may be accessible to AOL members and only after they have logged into the AOL site. If AOL wished to have a dispute resolution service, as it very well may, it has several choices. It can provide AOL subscribers with a special password that identifies them as AOL members and thus gains them access any time they wish to some external Web site. Or, the dispute resolution service could be integrated into the AOL site. A dispute resolution service is simply a software product. Once the product exists it can be duplicated, modified for different uses, and licensed. There can be "private label" ODR spaces if that is what a site owner wishes to have.

The Web has been a relatively free and open place. There is a saying, traceable back to the Web's early days, that "on the Internet, information wants to be free." Much information and many sites are, and will continue to be, accessible at no cost. But it does not have to be that way. Technically, levels of permissions can be designed that are limited only by the creativity of a programmer. There have already been a huge number of online spaces created and whether these spaces are free or costly, open or restricted, convenient and trustworthy, or inconvenient with a high risk is a function of how the software code has been written.

Flexibility in configuring dispute resolution approaches online is both an opportunity and a challenge. The opportunity is that any business can, quite quickly, have its own "court" or, if it prefers, provide easy access of various kinds to external "courts." The challenge is that the choice of how easy access will be and how closely the ODR space will be identified with the sponsor can affect the independence and neutrality of the third party.

Any action that compromises the independence and neutrality of third parties diminishes their authority and effectiveness. There is a value, in other words, in promoting accessibility and yet trying to preserve some distance. The best way to handle this is to provide users with details of any relationship that exists between the Web site owner and the dispute resolution service. Is there a financial relationship between the Web site owner and the ODR service? Is dispute resolution subsidized by the Web site owner, or do fees or some other source cover the expense of the service?

Different marketplaces will face different kinds of challenges in explaining the relationship between the third party and the sponsoring Web site. In a marketplace like eBay, for example, SquareTrade.com acknowledges that dispute resolution is subsidized by eBay. Yet, it is the buyers and sellers who use eBay, not eBay itself, who are the parties in any dispute. A subsidy in this kind of marketplace is not a problem since it does not raise problems of neutrality. If an ISP were to have a dispute resolution site and were to subsidize the service, possibilities for impropriety would be greater. In these cases, clear acknowledgment of the subsidy and why the ODR service believes its neutrality would not be compromised, should be explained.

Basic Building Choices

What approaches would provide the most fluid process of interaction and exchange? What media should be employed and what should the appropriate balance be between reliance on technology and reliance on people? These questions will resurface more than once in later chapters, but here are a few of the issues that must be faced.

- *Synchronous versus asynchronous communication*—An example of synchronous communication would be a chat room or other "place" where all are "present" and interact at the same time. Examples of asynchronous communication would be email or Web-based exchanges where one communicates at a time that is most convenient.

- *Image versus text versus numbers versus video*—The medium may not be the message but media do affect the message. Videoconferencing would allow real-time interactions with many of the qualities of face-to-face meetings. Text has other virtues, in that complex ideas can be explained and details of agreements can be preserved. Images, particularly animated or colored graphics, can show patterns and changes over time.

- *Automated versus human interaction*—How much and what kind of reliance should be placed on interaction with a machine, and when should trained third parties be employed? How can machines be employed to enhance the skills of the third party and to work with the third party rather than in lieu of it?

Enhancing ODR Space

Choices involving all three of the above categories of issues will be present in any attempt to construct a dispute resolution space. These are mostly choices about the manner in which exchanges should take place, and they will lead to considerable differences in ODR approaches. A further, and very significant, difference in sites will be a result of the degree to which information is processed as well as communicated.

Until a year or two ago, most Web sites were simply collections of files that were stored on a server. Clicking on a link meant that one of these files would appear on your screen. Anyone else who clicked on the same link would see the same information on their screen. Such Web sites are easy to set up, and costs for hosting them, if you do not own your own server, are relatively low.

More recently, it has become likely that clicking on a link will bring you something that will be different from what other people clicking on the same link will receive. This occurs because the server either knows something about you or you have been able to provide some specific criteria about the information that you want. Web servers are increasingly machines that not only store files that are sent whole to users but are machines that contain applications that collect information, assess it, and respond to requests for discrete data.

The simplest information processing of this sort occurs when one fills out an online form and clicks "submit." If I wish to purchase a new computer, I can go to a manufacturer's Web site and see a form on which I can select a processor speed, hard disk size, video monitor, sound card, and various other features. When I press "submit," I see on the screen, a few seconds later, what the configuration I want will cost.

More complex information processing occurs as information is obtained about users in more sophisticated ways. Network computers can be silent observers that keep track of one's online behavior and see patterns of behavior over time. If I have made several airline reservations to San Francisco over the past few months, the next time I go to the travel site that I use it may alert me to any reduced airfares there might be to San Francisco. This may be a convenience to me. It is also a situation that raises many privacy concerns, since I may not want my travel patterns to be available to others without explicitly giving my permission first.

Dynamic Web sites, ones that collect and process information as well as store it, have flexibility in interacting with users that static sites do not have. They can direct certain information to some users and not to other users. They can provide "feedback" about a transaction that assures the user that the action actually took place. Most generally, information processing can add new levels of convenience by anticipating user needs and can contribute to trust building by monitoring the process and enhancing communication among all the participants.

Increasing convenience and trust are critically important goals in any online process, but information processing will also challenge skills and decision making. As just one relatively simple example, information processing allows great choice over how to present information to disputants. Would something be clearer if it were in the form of a table or graph, or presented in color rather than black and white? Once data are in electronic form, their manner of presentation can be altered quickly. For many third parties, there may be some new skills that will be needed. Those third parties that wish to employ their skills online will be challenged to expand their array of skills in various ways, but these new skills will probably also be increasingly useful in traditional face-to-face settings as well.

The next chapter reviews a decade of dispute resolution in cyberspace. Just as activity in general has accelerated greatly in the last year or two, so has ODR activity. Our consideration of what is needed to design an effective ODR space continues in Chapter Three.

2

A Brief History of ODR

Stage One: Pre-1995, *Listservs and Flaming, Changing Identities in Cyberspace, The Most Famous Early Dispute in Cyberspace;* **Stage Two: 1995–1998; Emerging Institutions: 1998 to the Present,** *Government and ODR, Blind Bidding Models, SmartSettle, Domain Name Disputes, SquareTrade;* **Beyond 2000.**

When we received our first email accounts in 1990, we were also given a detailed set of rules called an "Acceptable Use Policy." What surprised us most about these rules was the simple fact that they existed. A set of rules of this sort usually means that there have been problems serious enough or frequent enough to cause a policy to be developed. The mere existence of the policy, therefore, indicated to us that the Internet, even then, was not a conflict-free space.

One of the rules prohibited users from sending "chain letters." Obviously, it had occurred to a creative user that if chain letters worked with what was called "snail mail," they would also work, and work more quickly, with email. Since there was no financial cost to the sender of "chain emails," the number that might circulate was quite high. Our university, like other universities, banned the sending of electronic chain letters claiming that if large numbers of students started circulating chain emails, the computer system would be overloaded. It was not clear how valid this argument was, but what was clear was that as ease of use increased and as costs declined, all kinds of informational transactions and transaction-related disputes would appear.

The most interesting rule, we thought, was a rule prohibiting commercial activity on the system. It was, frankly, not easy to imagine what kind of problem associated with commercial activity had caused such a policy. The only easily used online resource we had in those days was simple email. There was no such thing as an email "attachment" and, therefore, even sending a file to anyone was fairly cumbersome. No one had heard of the World Wide Web, and "banner ads," "spamming," and "cybersquatting" were not yet part of the language of cyberspace. In terms of users, the Internet was populated mostly by faculty and students whose colleges or universities had Internet connections.

The prohibition of commercial activity, it turned out, did not originate with some problem involving users at our university. It was, instead, a rule for the whole Net, promulgated by the National Science Foundation, which at that time had responsibility for managing the Net. The Net, which had begun as a military project, had evolved into a system for fostering academic research and communication, and those who used and controlled the system did not wish to open it up to others or for other purposes.

In a little more than a decade, we have experienced growth at a scale and pace that no one could have reasonably predicted. Recently, as we recalled the days when there was no commerce at all on the Net, a request for assistance appeared on our Web site from a person in Australia. It seems that this person was involved in a dispute with a company in the United States. The person, it turned out, received money by placing a link to an "adult" site on his own Web site. Every time this link was clicked and a person was sent to the adult site, he was supposed to earn a small referral fee. Lately, however, he had not been receiving this fee. He was still trying to get the adult site to pay him what he was owed, but if his negotiations with the adult site were not successful, he wished to know whether we would be willing to be of assistance.

Although this was not the kind of dispute we had in mind when we began thinking about online conflict, we would have been willing to assist him. Fortunately, we did not have to do this because he was able to resolve the dispute by himself. But it did make it clear to us how much had changed in ten years. There were now huge numbers of people around the globe who had easy and cheap access to the Internet. The possibility for making money had grown from sending chain emails to almost anything that one could think of. The interactions that were taking place had reached a scale and variety that was hard to comprehend. And there were still large numbers of people in many different locations who had not yet become participants in cyberspace.

This chapter presents a brief historical overview of online dispute resolution. This is useful information for you as you consider how you are going to utilize ODR processes. This history can be divided into three main time periods. The first, lasting until approximately 1995, was a period in which disputes arose and dispute resolution was applied informally and in particular contexts. There were not large numbers of disputes, but there were some very interesting and noteworthy ones. Various online mechanisms were employed to deal with these conflicts, but there were no organized dispute resolution institutions that were devoted specifically to ODR.

During a second period, from 1995 to 1998, recognition grew that the Net needed some focused online institutions to address problems that were arising with some frequency. Various experimental projects, largely university-based and foundation-funded, attempted to address these conflicts. Some of these efforts continue and much was learned even from the ones that have gone out of existence.

The period since 1998 has been one in which an ODR industry has begun to emerge. There has been recognition by governmental and commercial interests that online resources can be a solution to many problems that originate in the online environment. Unlike three or four years ago, it is now accepted that it is appropriate, indeed desirable, for ODR to be the process of first choice for disputes generated in online activities. It has also been recognized that technologies that work for online disputes can be efficiently employed for offline disputes, as well.

Of the three time periods, the first lasted the longest—almost half a decade—while the third was the shortest. Yet, more has probably occurred in the last two years even though it was the briefest of the time periods. We are in a period of accelerated change with new institutions appearing faster than before and also becoming obsolete faster than before. The year 2000 was an extraordinary one for ODR, but we have no doubt that the pace of change will accelerate even more.

Stage One: Pre-1995

Although most people when they first encounter email use it first for sending a message to a single individual, email can also be used to reach large numbers of people. This can happen in a variety of ways. Any email message can be easily and quickly forwarded to others, who may then forward it to more people, and so forth. These are, in a sense, unintentional chain letters because what began as one email can, fairly quickly, be passed along and end up in many email boxes.

Email grew in use because it was both an efficient mode of one-to-one communication and an equally efficient one-to-many and many-to-many form of communication, as well. The most familiar one-to-many or many-to-many vehicle was the "listserv." Anyone who subscribed to a listserv could send an email message to a single address, and then it was automatically forwarded to all the subscribers. Thousands of listservs grew up around every imaginable topic. In some of these listservs, new subscribers had to be approved, and a moderator had authority to approve every message that was circulated. More commonly, anyone with an interest in the topic could subscribe and send messages.

Listservs and Flaming

Listservs were the forum in which the most common conflict of the early 1990s took place. While most discussions on most listservs were conducted following a form of good behavior labeled "netiquette," many disagreements deteriorated into "flaming," defined as writing messages that were "particularly nasty, personal attacks on somebody for something he or she has written."[1] Flaming tended to cause what may have been a difference of opinion to escalate, often bringing in people on the listserv who were not involved in the original exchanges.[2]

The people who were probably most active in online dispute resolution in the early 1990s were the listserv moderators who needed to use their powers of persuasion whenever a "flame war" began and angry and rude messages began filling up email boxes and interfering with the interests of most subscribers. We have fortunately not been the targets of any flames, but the need for listserv owners to have dispute resolution skills became apparent to us in early 1994.

In March 1994, we organized a listserv that would allow discussion of issues related to dispute resolution. The list, called "dispute-res,"[3] now more than six years old and with almost a thousand subscribers, has been a model of polite and civil discourse. The most notable exception happened the very first week the list was in existence when a subscriber submitted messages attacking a professor at some university who, it was alleged, had treated the subscriber unfairly and caused great harm to his academic career. The messages were intemperate as well as accusatory, and potentially libelous. What should one do?

Listserv owners have the power to unsubscribe anyone. This would have been the simplest action to take to end the emails this subscriber was sending as well as the host of responding emails that attacked this person for the messages he was sending. By doing so, however, we would probably have provoked someone on the list to accuse us of abusing our authority, and thus cause a new dispute to erupt. More importantly, while we could remove a subscriber, we could not prevent him from resubscribing under a different name or address. A big part of the problem in such situations involves the messages sent by others; they are always an attempt to help, but they end up making the problem worse because they increase the number of messages being circulated and often provoke further responses from persons who were not involved earlier. The most effective strategy, therefore, is almost always for the listserv owner to simply urge other participants not to respond at all and hope that the offending subscriber will get tired and go away.

If the problematic messages are totally off-topic this usually works, since other subscribers will categorize the person as a nuisance—a kind of background noise. Much more challenging are situations in which a subscriber participates in a discussion that is taking place but does so in a rude, hostile, and inappropriate manner. Exercising the power that a listserv owner has to unsubscribe such a person will inevitably bring charges that you are infringing on free speech rights. In many cases, some direct private communication with the person about how the manner of expression is lowering the quality of the discussion may be necessary and will generally be effective.

It was, we thought, particularly ironic that a list oriented around alternative dispute resolution would encounter a serious conflict almost at its birth. We like to think that our mediation experience enabled us to end this conflict fairly quickly, but it was largely by not intervening, rather than intervening, that this and most other, listserv-based disputes were ended.

Listserv-based disputes tended to be angry and emotional, but they were almost always handled within the listserv. These were groups in which subscribers came to understand which subscribers were most prone to attacking others, and hostile remarks would be responded to less when coming from a particular source. In some instances, large numbers of the group rather than the list owner expressed ongoing disagreement with someone so often, that the person, while not formally expelled, would finally leave, not trying to return under another name.

Changing Identities in Cyberspace

While the pre-1995 online environment did not generate a broad variety of disputes, some of the most interesting cyberspace disputes did arise during that period. One kind of dispute that often still plagues us today concerns the use of identities that mislead others about who you are. What may still be the most famous dispute of this kind occurred on an online system called Compuserve in the early 1980s.

While Internet Service Providers today offer Internet access for a few dollars a month and in some situations provide access for free, there were no Internet Service Providers in the 1980s or at the beginning of the 1990s. For those not affiliated with a university, the main options for online communication were several companies running private networks. Compuserve was the largest of these, and one could use a modem to dial and connect to the Compuserve system and participate in discussions with other Compuserve subscribers. Only at a later point did it become possible for email to move between the Internet and the private systems. Compuserve, which is now owned by AOL, was an early model for AOL, and for a few years, AOL and Compuserve were each other's main competitor.

What has become known as "The Case of the Electronic Lover" involved a discussion group on Compuserve and a participant named Joan. Joan claimed to be a New York neuropsychologist who had been severely disfigured in an automobile accident. She was confined to a wheelchair but was able to type and participate in Compuserve discussions. Joan had a "sassy, bright, generous personality in a medium where physicality doesn't count."[4] Joan was highly admired, often helping others with serious disabilities.

Some time later it was revealed that Joan was not a neuropsychologist and had not been in a serious automobile accident. She was also not a woman. Joan turned out to be a psychiatrist in New York named Alex who claimed that he was trying to understand what it felt like to be female and experience the nature of friendships among women.

Many participants in the Compuserve discussion were upset at the deception, but it was not altogether clear whether or how she had hurt them. "Joan" was not who she said she was, and she was able to elicit information from women participants that would not have been revealed to a man. But it is difficult to fit parts of this dispute into categories we are familiar with. We have never before had a medium in which it was as easy to do what "Joan" did as it is on the Internet.

Identity is still an issue that is part of many disputes. What should we have to reveal about ourselves, and how can we be certain who we are interacting with? "The Case of the Electronic Lover" raised the consciousness of many people about the care that should be taken in interacting with strangers online, but this is an ongoing issue, particularly for new users of the Internet. Many ISPs do have rules that might be applied to behavior such as "Joan's." But we are still struggling with a large variety of issues involving anonymity and privacy.

The Most Famous Early Dispute in Cyberspace

Many people online have more email addresses than they have physical addresses. Having different email addresses is a little like having different identities for different activities. In different contexts online, we may want to communicate only a part of who we are. If nothing else, cyberspace gives us more flexibility than we have in the physical world for creating identities.

The issue of online privacy involves one side of the identity issue. While we can create multiple identities, there are also technological means for others to learn who is behind these identities. We are often asked to create "user names" for ourselves in order to enter some online space. Yet, if we do not reveal enough information about ourselves for the Web site owner to acquire some information about who we are, where we live, and whether or not we can be linked to some credit card or payment system, we may not be allowed to participate in whatever it is that is being offered.

One place where there was complete flexibility about hiding one's identity was an online "place" called LambdaMOO. While "Joan" participated in a forum where one *could* create an identity, LambdaMOO was a place where one was *required* to create an identity. Using this identity, one could enter LambdaMOO: an environment that users thought of as a large house. There were many rooms in this house and users moved from room to room by typing various commands. One could do anything one wanted to do in a room, also by typing commands on the keyboard.

What was novel about LambdaMOO is that one could do things in it that the laws of physics might not allow to be done in the real world. LambdaMOO was a fantasy world that could be inhabited by people anywhere, and the house expanded to accommodate whatever number of people were "present." In addition, one could place objects into any room and the objects could do anything the creator wanted them to do, even if this required supernatural powers.

One night in March 1993, a person whose identity in LambdaMOO was Mr. Bungle, created a voodoo doll in the living room and used the voodoo doll to coerce two of the room's occupants to engage in violent sex acts. Even when Mr. Bungle was ejected from the room, he was able to use the voodoo doll from other rooms. Finally, "someone summoned Iggy, a wise and trusted old-timer who brought with him a gun of near wizardly powers, a gun that didn't kill but enveloped its targets in a cage impermeable even to a voodoo doll's powers."[5] Then Iggy fired his gun at Mr. Bungle, thus ending the episode.

Participants in LambdaMOO took this incident very seriously and after lengthy discussions about what kind of act Mr. Bungle had actually committed and whether he caused real harm, and what kind of place LambdaMOO was, Mr. Bungle was removed from the system. The incident also occasioned the development of an arbitration system to deal with disputes among participants. Arbitrators came from LambdaMOO participants and dealt with cases involving property, such as who owns objects that are created in LambdaMOO, and speech, such as the use of "violent verbs."

LambdaMOO was an interesting online community that came to believe that it needed some formal structures and processes to deal with conflict that emerged there. What LambdaMOO did not do or even consider was to look outside of itself for an ODR provider who might have brought more expertise to the disputes that were occurring. One reason for this, of course, was that such projects did not really exist and, as we shall describe in the next section, only began to emerge in 1996 and 1997.

Stage Two: 1995–1998

Justice Oliver Wendell Holmes once wrote that "the life of the law is not logic, it is experience."[6] The history of conflict and conflict resolution on the Internet is clearly connected to experience. The early experience of the Internet, for example, involved users in academic settings. Not surprisingly, therefore, many online disputes involved colleges and universities or college students.

Mr. Bungle, described in the previous section, was a student at New York University. In another highly publicized case, a University of Michigan student named Jake Baker was prosecuted for sending a short story he had written to an Internet newsgroup.[7] The story had descriptions of violence occurring to a character with the same name as a student in one of Baker's classes. In another case, an MIT student named David Lamacchia used his MIT computer account to make available copyrighted software; he was prosecuted by federal authorities.[8]

In the mid-1990s, more people began using the Internet and in many new ways. In September 1994, the Federal Trade Commission (FTC) filed its first case accusing someone of committing fraud online.[9] The case involved an America Online subscriber named Brian Corzine who advertised the following:

—"FOR JUST $99.00 WE WILL SHOW YOU HOW TO CREATE A BRAND NEW CREDIT FILE AT ALL 3 OF THE MAJOR CREDIT BUREAUS . . . 100% LEGAL AND 200% GUARANTEED."

As a result of the FTC action, Corzine agreed to stop advertising credit repair programs and to provide compensation to consumers.

Also in the mid-1990s, conflicts began to arise involving Internet Service Providers (ISPs). What rights and responsibilities did they have when, for example, subscribers used their accounts to distribute copyrighted software? Did the ISP have to check accounts to see if any illegal activity was occurring? Did the ISP have any liability if accounts were used for illegal purposes? Under what circumstances could ISPs terminate subscriptions? In late 1995, a group met in Washington, D.C. to see if they could design an online system that would allow some of the conflicts involving ISPs to be resolved online and to be resolved quickly. This was the beginning of the Virtual Magistrate.

The Virtual Magistrate was conceived of by David Johnson, a lawyer in Washington who was one of the earliest and most creative thinkers about law and cyberspace. In early 1996, a private foundation called the National Center for Automated Information Research (NCAIR), decided to provide grants for several experimental ODR projects. The first of these was the Virtual Magistrate. In a second set of grants, NCAIR provided funding for the Online Ombuds Office, a project we had proposed, and for a family law mediation project at the University of Maryland.

In addition to the grants, NCAIR organized a conference on Online Dispute Resolution in May 1996 and commissioned papers on various topics related to ODR.[10] These papers are not only an interesting historical archive, but they discuss structures and approaches for ODR that are still relevant today. None of the

writers anticipated the entrepreneurial efforts we have been wit-
nessing recently, but the value of ODR and reasons why ODR was
most appropriate for disputes arising online were recognized.

The three projects that were funded presented three different
opportunities for experimentation.

- The Virtual Magistrate Project was an arbitration project. It is
  often viewed as having been unsuccessful because only one
  case was arbitrated. It still exists, however, as a project at the
  Chicago-Kent College of Law[11] and may begin to receive
  more cases. What was most instructive about the Virtual
  Magistrate was what it indicated about the use of arbitration
  online. We shall discuss and compare online arbitration with
  online mediation later, but a clear lesson learned was that it is
  difficult if there is no prior agreement to persuade the
  respondent to participate in arbitration. An Internet Service
  Provider or other respondent usually will see no reason to
  agree in advance to a ruling by an arbitrator.

- The Online Ombuds Office was a mediation project. We have
  been more successful than the Virtual Magistrate in attracting
  cases because parties were told that the process was voluntary
  and that they could leave at any time. One of the lessons we
  learned was that working through and affiliating with
  marketplaces is an effective way, even with mediation, to
  improve rates at which respondents agree to participate. What
  was clear from the beginning was that the interaction
  between mediators and disputants would be enhanced as new
  software was developed. Many of the new ODR ventures that
  we shall discuss in the next section have been working on
  this.

- Unlike the Virtual Magistrate Project and the Online
  Ombuds Office, the Maryland Family Mediation project was
  focused on a particular type of dispute. Many family disputes
  can be dealt with on an issue-by-issue basis and, most
  importantly, there are many family disputes that involve

parties in different locations. If the parents are separated by distance, ODR could be a fruitful method of resolving problems. The Maryland project also did not attract many cases but we have begun to see just the kind of cases that Richard Granat, who conceived of the project, envisioned.[12]

This period saw the emergence of other experiments, such as the Cybertribunal project at the University of Montreal Faculty of Law. Cybertribunal has evolved into a commercial venture called eResolution and is involved both with online mediation and online arbitration. It is one of the accredited providers of arbitration for domain name disputes that we shall discuss in the next section. Looking back on the period of 1995–1998, it is clear that in several places at about the same time, the need and value of ODR became apparent. That was a period in which there were far fewer users of cyberspace and in which electronic commerce had not yet taken hold. Yet, it was a period in which ideas and approaches that currently underlie ODR started to be explored.

Emerging Institutions: 1998 to the Present

The pioneering efforts of the mid-1990s were imaginative first steps. The organizers were clearly correct in believing that as the Web matured, online civic institutions would be needed. These projects remain important reference points for anyone beginning an ODR project today. Yet, unlike most recent ODR endeavors, these tended not to be commercial endeavors, and they provide little understanding of what is necessary to sustain ventures that do not rely on academic, philanthropic, or governmental support.

The most recent period has been characterized by significant entrepreneurial activity and strong interest and support by high-level governmental and corporate bodies. In addition, the traditional ADR community has begun focusing on ODR and its significance for lawyers, arbitrators, and mediators. We are in quite an interesting period in which disputes have been surfacing, demand for ODR has been growing, and in which effective ODR systems have emerged. The future growth of ODR is tied to creating links between those who have disputes and those who have solutions. This has begun and as it progresses further, ODR will be a much more widely used and available option for the growing number of online users.

This section reviews the nature of governmental and corporate activity in support of ODR and examines four of the more interesting, active, and ambitious ODR ventures (see Appendix 1 for a more comprehensive list). These are:

- The "blind bidding" solutions used mainly in insurance company claims.
- SmartSettle, a sophisticated negotiation system that guarantees better solutions than parties could reach themselves.
- The online arbitration process established for disputes between trademark owners and domain name owners.
- The large-scale online mediations handled by a private company, SquareTrade, for several online marketplaces.

Government and ODR

In June 1999, the Federal Trade Commission held a workshop on the subject of "U.S. Perspectives on Consumer Protection in the Global Electronic Marketplace."[13] The FTC had observed that the "number of direct, international business-to-consumer transactions involving electronic commerce is expected to increase significantly in the future" and that the rate of growth of online consumer transactions might be slowed ". . . until consumers develop confidence in commercial activities conducted over global networks and businesses are assured of a stable and predictable commercial environment. Accordingly, the present challenge is to encourage the development of a global marketplace that offers safety, transparency, and legal certainty."

The FTC solicited comments and suggestions in advance of the meeting and indicated that one issue of concern was "to what extent is there a need for international dispute resolution procedures or tribunals for consumers engaged in electronic commerce with foreign businesses." Aside from our own submission, almost no mention of ODR was made in any of the more than sixty comments submitted. Yet, early in the meeting, the first question asked by an FTC commissioner was how online dispute resolution could be employed to assist consumers with problems arising out of online purchases. This question placed a small blip on the radar screen of those engaged in and concerned with electronic commerce. During the next year, the small blip grew rapidly, and one year later, in June, 2000, the FTC joined with the Department of Commerce to sponsor a two-day workshop exclusively on the topic of ODR.[14] The summary report issued by the FTC highlighted the following:

- *Finding global solutions to address global transactions:* This process is already underway. Several companies are pursuing multilingual ADR mechanisms and international partnerships for conducting ADR. Some businesses, consumer groups, and governments have already begun cooperative activities in the ADR field.

- *Pursuing technological innovation:* The workshop showcased the dozens of emerging ADR providers that have taken advantage of various technologies to provide new options to consumers. Participants agreed that industry should continue to develop new ADR programs in consultation with consumer groups and to report to governments on their development.

- *Pursuing multiple ADR programs:* The workshop demonstrated that "one size does not fit all" and that participants should work together to create different types of ADR programs suitable for different types of disputes. Already a variety of programs are developing, including blind bidding systems, online mediation, and online arbitration.

- *Ensuring fairness and effectiveness of ADR programs:*
  Participants agreed that stakeholders should work together to
  ensure that ADR programs are fair and effective. In ensuring
  fairness and effectiveness, stakeholders should make sure that
  ADR programs are impartial, free or low-cost, accessible,
  transparent, and quick. Participants disagreed on some
  specifics of these elements and how they operate in practice.
  Workshop discussions also suggested that there should be a
  balance between fairness and effectiveness. For example, if too
  many procedural rules were added to a program in an attempt
  to make it fair, the program could be too expensive to be
  effective. Several groups such as the American Arbitration
  Association, the European Commission, and the Better
  Business Bureau are working to promote fairness and
  effectiveness by developing codes of conduct for online ADR.

- *Consumer and business education:* Participants agreed that all
  stakeholders should work together to promote consumer and
  business education about seal programs, codes of conduct, and
  ADR. Forums such as the Department of Commerce and FTC
  ADR workshop can go a long way toward understanding
  emerging ADR systems, exploring the many difficult issues
  in this area, and publicizing the availability of ADR for
  businesses and consumers.

- *Action against fraudulent and deceptive practices related to ADR:*
  Companies have expressed their support for working with law
  enforcement to combat fraudulent and deceptive ADR
  practices. Discussions are under way for ADR providers to
  refer complaints to law enforcement agencies.[15]

In addition to the FTC and Department of Commerce workshop, cross-border disputes involving consumers were the topic of
several other meetings and conferences. These included a conference sponsored by the Global Business Dialogue, a group of corporate executives from major E-commerce companies,[16] a jointly
sponsored meeting on "Building Trust in the Online Environment:

Business-to-Consumer Dispute Resolution," organized by the Organisation for Economic Co-operation and Development (OECD), the Hague Conference on Private International Law (HCPIL), and the International Chamber of Commerce (ICC), and a meeting jointly arranged by the World Intellectual Property Organization, the London Court of International Arbitration (LCIA), the Dispute Resolution Section of the American Bar Association (ABA), the Singapore Subordinate Courts, and the Swiss Arbitration Association (ASA) on the Organization for Economic Co-operation and Development.[17] These conferences produced a wealth of material about ODR that is accessible on the Web.

While these conferences highlighted a fair amount of agreement on the need to protect consumers who purchase items from a seller in another jurisdiction, they did not focus very much attention on the value of ODR in other kinds of disputes and contexts. In a later section we shall discuss how, during the next few years, ODR is likely to be employed in a broadening range of situations.

Blind Bidding Models

Blind bidding systems allow parties in a dispute to submit settlement offers to a computer, and if the offers are within a certain range, often 30 percent, of each other, the parties agree to settle and split the difference. What is attractive about blind bidding is that if no settlement is reached, the offers are never revealed to the other party. This is intended to encourage parties to be more truthful about what their "bottom line" might be.

Blind bidding can be looked at as a negotiation tool, something employed to give negotiators an option that, at best, was a cumbersome option previously. Yet, blind bidding can also be viewed as a process in which a computer becomes a neutral third party that accepts the offers submitted to it and does not reveal the offers to the other parties. The machine evaluates each offer to see whether it is within the 30 percent range. If so, the parties are informed that there is a settlement. If not, no information about the offers is revealed to the parties.

Thus far, blind bidding has been employed almost exclusively in claims against insurance companies. These are claims that are generally settled at some point, but the process that has been employed traditionally, involving personal injury lawyers and insurance claim adjusters, can be lengthy and inefficient. There are problems with the parties and their representatives playing "phone tag" and posturing in ways that often take up time. There certainly could be a human third party who accepted the offers in a manner similar to how the computer accepts offers. This is occasionally done but never as efficiently as the way blind bidding systems employ the network.

These systems are impressive, but they are also extremely limited. They are efficient, but, at least currently, they only work with disputes where a single variable is contested. This variable must also be one that uses numbers so that the machine can make the necessary calculations. The insurance context is a perfect first arena for blind bidding because differences often focus exclusively on money, and the existing system is both expensive and inefficient.[18]

There are a growing number of blind bidding companies, most notably Cybersettle and ClicknSettle. The underlying technology in blind bidding is not very complex and costs of entry to anyone wishing to start a company using a form of blind bidding are not high. There are, of course, costs of marketing and of obtaining business, and there may be differences in certain details. Some systems may require representation by counsel and others not. Some may allow unlimited bids and others not. Some may allow bids in ranges and others not. It is possible for companies to differentiate themselves from other blind bidding systems, but they all are built on the same basic concept.

The future of blind bidding will inevitably broaden beyond insurance company disputes. In many mediations or arbitrations there may have been many differences at the start but only a monetary issue at the end. Blind bidding technology could be helpful in such situations. In other situations, it might be desirable to offer blind bidding as an option before beginning a lengthier process. Blind bidding is a tool and can be injected into any phase of a dispute resolution process. OnlineResolution.com, for example, offers blind bidding as a standard feature in its "Resolution Room" process, considering it to be one out of many possible tools that a mediator might employ.

SmartSettle

SmartSettle,[19] originally called OneAcccord, is much more sophisticated negotiation software than the blind bidding systems. SmartSettle is intended for use in disputes that are simple or complex, single-issue or multi-issue, two-party or multiparty, composed of quantitative or qualitative issues, of short or long duration, and involving interdependent factors and issues. SmartSettle has been enhanced over the last few years, and, like any software, succeeding versions are both more powerful and less complex than prior versions. SmartSettle will never be as easy to use as blind bidding, and may not be needed for common and relatively simple consumer transactions. Yet, more than any other software, SmartSettle takes advantage of the power of the network to bring disputants solutions that may not have been apparent to them.

SmartSettle works by having disputants move through several stages, each of which clarifies what is at issue in the dispute, how strongly the parties feel about the different issues, and what ranges of outcomes might be acceptable. This information is placed on a "single negotiating form" which parties use to fashion proposals and, it is hoped, reach agreement. In the early phases, SmartSettle provides a structure for issue clarification and assessment that, by itself, can help parties reach consensus. What is most novel about SmartSettle, however, is that it can take any tentative agreement and suggest alternative approaches that give each party more than they were willing to accept in the settlement that had been agreed to.

Domain Name Disputes

The Internet is a network of computers that can exchange information. In order to do this, every machine connected to the Internet is identified with a unique string of numbers called an IP (Internet Protocol) address. The IP address, something like 128.119.199.27 for a machine on the University of Massachusetts campus, is all that machines on the network need to get email to the right place or to allow a World Wide Web user to access a particular Web site.

Unfortunately, human beings are not as comfortable as machines are in using numbers. So, to facilitate use by humans, the domain name system was developed. With domain names, one can access the University of Massachusetts Web site by remembering "www.umass.edu" rather than 128.119.199.27. Until 1998, the domain name system was managed by the U.S. government or by companies to which the government delegated authority. In 1998, management and supervision of the domain name system was turned over to the Internet Corporation for Assigned Names and Numbers (ICANN), a nonprofit corporation established solely for the purpose of maintaining the domain name system.

The domain name system arose with little thought given to the disputes that might be caused by it. Domain names had little value before the Internet began to be used for commercial purposes, and for most of the history of the Internet, there was no need for a process to resolve domain name disputes. Eventually, however, companies began to realize that a domain name they might wish to have had already been registered by someone else. In an early dispute, for example, a journalist registered the domain name "McDonalds.com" before the McDonalds fast food chain.

The response of those companies that wished to obtain a domain name that had already been registered was to claim that trademark law had been violated. Trademark law lets citizens and businesses own parts of our language. Trademark law creates property interests in words and in letter combinations that are not words. "eBay" and "Exxon" are not in the dictionary, but they are owned by companies and others cannot use these marks.

Domain names allow an individual or an organization exclusive control over some piece of cyberspace. Only one company can have the "McDonalds.com" domain name. In the physical world, businesses doing different things can use the same word, for example, "McDonalds," since there will be no confusion between a McDonalds selling shoes and a McDonalds selling hamburgers. In cyberspace, the use of one domain name by multiple entities causes problems.

Domain names can be registered by anyone and the cost is quite nominal. Those in charge of registering domain names could have avoided some conflict by making registrants aware that they might have a problem if they registered a word that was trademarked. There is even a Web site run by the U.S. Patent and Trademark Office that allows the trademark database to be searched for free.[20] This was never done, however, and, even today, anyone who wishes to register a word that is trademarked can do so. Whatever problems might arise will have to be faced later.

After ICANN took over management of the domain name system, it put in place a process for resolving some domain name disputes. The ICANN Uniform Dispute Resolution Policy (UDRP) provides trademark holders with a process that is faster and less expensive than litigation.[21] The UDRP, however, is not mandatory, nor is it binding, arbitration. Trademark holders can still go to court instead of using the UDRP, and the party that loses the arbitration can go to court after the decision is handed down. Court cases, however, are relatively few compared to the number of disputes handled through the UDRP.

In the first year of the ICANN process, from December 1999 to December 2000, approximately twenty-five hundred complaints were filed with almost three-quarters of the decisions being made in favor of the complainant or trademark holder. There has been considerable criticism of the UDRP and calls to revise it. Even so, it is a significant example of an ODR process that has been able to resolve a substantial number of cases.

SquareTrade

SquareTrade is probably the most ambitious recent Internet ODR start-up. It began in February 2000 and as of early December 2000, had handled over thirty thousand disputes, most of which probably originated in transactions at the online auction site eBay. Square-Trade has agreements to be the dispute resolution provider for over a dozen marketplaces, the largest of which is eBay. eBay is an environment in which approximately five million items are for sale at any one time, and two million transactions take place each week.

SquareTrade, in many ways, is a classic Internet start-up. Its founders are Harvard Business School graduates who worked for several years at the management consulting firm McKinsey and Co. We have had the privilege of advising SquareTrade since its founding, and at least some of the ideas presented in this book have been implemented by SquareTrade.

SquareTrade is notable because it has demonstrated that it is possible to "scale up" and efficiently handle large numbers of disputes. It has been able to do this by designing a two-stage process: a free negotiation process with no human third party, and, if that is unsuccessful, an online mediation process with a human mediator. Most disputes, however, are resolved in the first stage, and this accounts for the ability to manage a large caseload. By refining the direct negotiation process, success rates have risen from 40 percent to 60 percent and, as of December 2000, over 80 percent.

SquareTrade, along with BBBOnLine and WebAssured.com, offers a seal or trustmark that sellers can put on their Web sites. These seals should raise the level of trust and the willingness potential users have to use a particular Web site. Most merchants on the Web are small businesses and do not have a recognizable brand name. By displaying a seal, the Web site owner indicates that he has agreed to observe various requirements of the seal issuer. The SquareTrade seal commits a merchant to participation in a dispute resolution process if a problem occurs, to abide by a series of responsible business practices,[22] and, in addition, SquareTrade provides fraud insurance. All of these seals help the merchant as much as the consumer because they should raise the willingness of anyone to transact business at the site. As we shall discuss in the next chapter, building trust is difficult in the online environment, and a seal or trustmark is one way to build trust without relying on word of mouth from satisfied users.

Beyond 2000

In November 1995, four Cornell University freshmen sent an email message to a few friends containing "Seventy-Five Reasons Why Women (Bitches) Should Not Have Freedom of Speech." Some of those who received the message soon forwarded it to others. Fairly quickly, the list was widely available on the Internet, leading to many cries for Cornell to severely punish the students and to other cries for Cornell to respect the students' rights of free expression. The students were neither expelled nor let off completely.[23]

In December 2000, the Internet was abuzz with the story of Claire and Brad, one a lawyer in London and the other an employee of a British Internet Service Provider. Claire had sent Brad an email explicitly describing sexual behavior they had engaged in. Brad, for whatever reason, sent a copy to some friends. It spread, first leading to stories in the British press and then to Web sites devoted to the story and the couple. On December 20, the lead story on the Microsoft home page was "Racy e-mail hits world."

Had anything changed in five years?

The same day we learned of the Brad and Claire story, a colleague asked us what he should do about a small problem he had encountered. He was taking his family on a short vacation and had made hotel reservations over the phone. Earlier that day, he looked up the hotel Web site and saw that the hotel was offering the same accommodations for fifty dollars a day less than what he had been quoted. When he called the hotel, the reservations office claimed to be completely unaware of anything on the Web site but agreed to lower his room rate by twenty dollars. He told them that he was holding a printout of the Web prices in his hand, but, of course, there was no way he could show the price list to the people on the other end of the phone. He didn't want to cancel his reservation, but he was annoyed.

We suggested that he take the printout with him and see whether an old-fashioned face-to-face encounter could bring him a lower price. But we also recognized that while this dispute was not in any way newsworthy, it was representative of a most important change that had occurred in the online environment in the last five years. Very simply, five years ago there would have been no such dispute because hotels were not yet routinely posting their rates online. A 1995 dispute involving email and college students was indicative of who was using the Web five years ago and how it was being used. Our colleague's conflict involving the Web and a commercial transaction was indicative of how the range of activities one might engage in online had broadened.

The Web has undergone extraordinary growth and change during the past five years, but it is quite probable that there will be equally great growth and change during the next five years. Whether the stock market goes up or down, whether particular companies are successful or not, there is little doubt that use of the Internet will increase, the number of people online will grow, and the range of activities for which people use the Internet will broaden.

In the United States, the number of persons online in December 1995 was fewer than twenty-five million. By December 2000, it was over one hundred and fifty million, with over 56 percent of U.S. households having Internet access.[24] It would be impossible for the number of U.S. households to increase sixfold again during the next five years, but it is not impossible for the total number of households and offices with Internet access to increase by another hundred million. It would also not be impossible for Internet access outside the U.S. to grow by several hundred million. Indeed, a recent study indicated that the number of Internet users in Asia would quadruple to 188 million by 2004.[25]

Growth in numbers has been joined by growth in the kinds of activities possible to engage in online, by more crossing over of the boundary between the online world and the offline world, and by more interaction among those for whom contact was previously limited by national and territorial boundaries. It is not possible to predict the rate of growth of the Internet, but even conservative estimates do not question the scale and nature of growth over time. Yet, if the need for ODR arises out of problems occurring with transactions and relationships, both online and offline, none of the numbers already cited captures the level of growth that is likely to occur in the next few years. The reason for this lies in the concept of "network effects," which assumes that the value of a network grows in proportion to the number of users. Stated most simply, networks with many users are worth more than networks with fewer users. Therefore, incentives to join any network will grow as the number of users grow.

But how much additional value is created by adding users, and what impact will adding users likely have on transactions and relationships? Bob Metcalfe, the inventor of Ethernet, has pointed out that one thousand people on a network can have roughly one million different conversations if everyone communicates with everyone else. Two thousand users, however, can have four million conversations. These cannot be considered precise predictions, but it is significant that adding a thousand users could result in millions of new interactions.

Even this, however, understates how rapidly growth can occur. Metcalfe's calculation shows what happens if each new user has some kind of relationship with every other user. But on the network, it is not only individuals who interact. Groups form and the groups also interact. Two-person groups, three-person groups, and much larger groups form with various combinations of people. This would suggest that even Metcalfe's calculation vastly underestimates how much of a catalyst new users and new applications are to relationships, transactions, and disputes.

Louis Gerstner, the chairman and CEO of IBM, has said that "inside IBM, we talk about ten times more connected people, one hundred times more network speed, one thousand times more devices, and a million times more data."[26] As we were writing this book in late 2000 and early 2001, the focus in the financial markets and in the news was on Internet and technology companies that were losing value. Providing dispute resolution services, like providing any online service, requires investment and resources, something that is not as easy to obtain as it was in 1999 or early 2000. Yet, the need for ODR can, we believe, only continue to grow, and the opportunities for applying ODR, as we shall discuss in later chapters, can only increase. The Internet is not a harmonious place, and at least some of the ventures mentioned in this chapter, or some new ventures, will be able to take advantage of that.

The landscape of online dispute resolution can be expected to grow and also become more crowded. Just as it took time for established offline companies to understand how important the Web was, the larger ADR organizations have been slower to see the relevance of ODR to their work. The most notable exception to this is the Better Business Bureau, which accepts complaints online and has seal programs for both reliability and privacy. What is clear at the end of 2000 that was not clear at the beginning of the year, is that major dispute resolution organizations such as the CPR Institute for Dispute Resolution, JAMS, and the American Arbitration Association have come to understand that ODR will inevitably be part of their future.

3

Understanding the ODR Process

The Fundamentals of ODR; The Convenience, Trust, and Expertise Triangle, *Convenience, When Parties Have Different Degrees of Access, The Issue of Record Keeping, Trust, The Trustworthiness of the Internet, An Example of Trust, Expertise, How Cyberspace Creates Process Options.*

Assume that the Internal Revenue Service sends you a notice stating that you owe an additional thousand dollars on your income taxes. To avoid additional problems, you are given twenty days to send in a check for this amount, plus interest, plus a penalty fee. You are quite surprised because you had been very careful in filling out your return. You read further and discover that they are disallowing a deduction you had taken for one of your dependents. They claim to have no record of your child with the social security number of 042-34-7845.

As you wonder about how this is possible, you notice that 042-34-7845 is not your child's social security number. The correct number is 042-34-7846. You find a copy of the return you filed, and indeed, you see that you did put in the incorrect number. What should you do?

The IRS notice indicates that you can send them a letter asking for a review or you can call an 800 number and speak to a person on the phone. It occurs to you that there should be a way to handle this electronically, either through email or a Web site where one could fill in a form explaining the error. The only options given to you, however, are telephone or snail mail. You choose the telephone, dial the number, hear eight options for dealing with different circumstances, choose one of them, are told that all the agents are busy and you should stay on the line, and then you wait thirty-five minutes until an agent comes on the line. You explain the problem and the agent says she will take care of it. She gives you her name, the case number, and says that within two weeks you will receive a letter from the IRS confirming what she has done.

If the IRS letter had said that you could communicate to the IRS via a Web site, would you have done so? Assuming that there was not only a Web site, but that the IRS had also decided that it would prefer that people use the Web site rather than telephone or snail mail, what could they have done to increase the chances that users would choose the Web site option?

At some point in the not too distant future, we will be able to interact online with government agencies. We can now search for and obtain information on the Web from most federal agencies, including the IRS. We can, if we wish, file tax returns electronically. But we cannot yet participate in their dispute resolution processes online. We are quite certain that we will be given online dispute resolution options in the future. But when we have such choices, what can be done to persuade us to use them?

The above scenario did not involve mediation or arbitration, but it was a typical kind of negotiation that will precede mediation or arbitration. If negotiation is successful, the dispute will evaporate and there will be no need for assistance from a third party. If negotiation fails, however, the need for mediation or arbitration will grow. We do not see any reason why a large number of dispute resolution processes involving government and citizens cannot take place online. We also believe that any dispute resolution process involving a potentially large caseload will not be used unless the approaches we suggest below are followed.

The Fundamentals of ODR

This chapter focuses on what we believe must be the three fundamental features or building blocks of any ODR system. These are the following:

- Convenience
- Trust
- Expertise

Very simply, no ODR system will be used or be successful unless it is convenient to use, provides a sense of trust and confidence in its use, and also delivers expertise. Described a little differently, such systems need to facilitate access and participation, have legitimacy, and provide value.

The challenge of ODR is not simply to provide some level of convenience, trust, and expertise, but to provide the right mix of convenience, trust, and expertise for users in particular contexts. Different people may have different needs or expectations for one or more of these factors. For example, what is sufficient trust for one will be insufficient for another. Whether trust is more important than the other factors and whether a high level of one factor can compensate for a low level of another will also be different for different people. Three things, however, are clear.

1. Everyone faced with a choice of whether to use an ODR system or process will make a calculation or assessment involving these three factors. It is this assessment that will determine whether one system will be used over another and whether online systems can compete effectively with offline systems.

2. Some measure of each of the factors must always be present. Every system must contain all the factors at some threshold or minimum level. Except for situations where one is compelled to participate and given no options at all, such as when one

receives a summons from a court, it will be rare that a high level of one factor can compensate for complete absence of another.

3. Threshold levels of all three factors must be met for all the parties. To do this may lead to providing less than desired levels for one or both parties.

The relationship between the three factors of convenience, trust, and expertise can be compared to the relationship between three sides of a triangle. In the convenience, trust, and expertise triangle (Figure 3.1), the length of each side represents how high a level of the factor is present. As with all triangles, our triangle of convenience, trust, and expertise can come in many different shapes because the length of each side can vary greatly as the level of one of these factors increases or decreases. What is necessary for the triangle to remain a triangle, or for the ODR system to be a legitimate ODR system, is for all these factors to be present in some measure.

The Convenience, Trust, and Expertise Triangle

In the IRS example, the choice of telephone over snail mail was probably made in a few seconds. We are used to assessing convenience, trust, and expertise frequently, routinely, and quickly. We all know our individual standards and expectations for convenience, trust, and expertise. If no other alternatives exist, one might choose a highly inconvenient system in which one has some measure of trust and which promises to deliver some measure of expertise. On the other hand, if some process does not seem to be "worth one's time and effort," or it appears illegitimate, or if there is reason to believe that those involved are incompetent, some other course of action will be chosen, ranging from, perhaps, going to court, to doing nothing.

The weights given to the three factors of convenience, trust, and expertise will vary among people and will also vary depending on context. If, for example, a problem is important to you and other

FIGURE 3.1 Convenience, Trust, and Expertise Triangle.

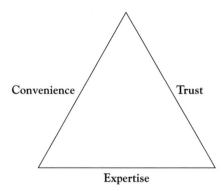

options are not present, you might participate in a process even if it is not very convenient. On the other hand, if the problem is not very important or is not very complex, you might be willing to work with a third party with less expertise than would be acceptable in a more complicated or important matter.

The IRS example is one in which the party had a choice of two offline methods to proceed. With offline disputes, ODR is likely to surface as an add-on to other already existing processes. There will then be a choice between ODR and ADR processes, and some assessment will have to be made of the relative amount of convenience, trust, and expertise provided by each dispute resolution process. For many disputes arising out of online activities, however, ODR will often be presented as the exclusive option. The choice will then be between participating or not participating, or between continuing to participate or leaving the dispute resolution process.

There is no objective way to measure the three factors to ascertain whether, in any particular ODR process, there is a sufficient amount of each. In any initial design of online dispute resolution processes, the challenge should be to do as much as possible to further the three goals of access and participation, legitimacy, and value, and, at a minimum, provide enough of each to meet some threshold level. We can expect that early versions of a system will bring relatively low levels of each factor. If the system is used and is even moderately successful, one can assume that threshold levels have been met. In subsequent versions, attention should be paid to trying to raise the levels of each.

These three factors are generally not independent of each other. In other words, if the level of one factor is changed, the level of some other factor may be affected. Raising one factor a lot may lower another factor a little—often a beneficial trade-off. Or, raising one factor a lot may, at the same time, also raise the level of some other factor—almost certainly a desirable outcome. What is challenging is that the impact of making changes in a system will vary on who the parties are and what the context is. There is often a trade-off between the power of an application (expertise) and how complicated it is to use (convenience). This may be a desirable course to take when training is feasible that can raise the convenience level for users. In other situations, the simplest system will be preferable, even if it is less powerful.

One very simple but useful way to visualize where the strengths and weaknesses of an ODR system are is to draw a triangle that you believe represents the ODR system. For example, if we were thinking about the ICANN dispute resolution process for domain names, we might draw the triangle in Figure 3.2. It makes the point that the process is fairly high on convenience, provides reasonable expertise, but something to do with trust, legitimacy, and fairness is quite weak.

On the other hand, a very powerful negotiation tool such as SmartSettle might suggest the triangle in Figure 3.3, where the expertise and trust levels are very high but usability might increase if the level of convenience were raised.

As you build your approach you should be interested in systems that will both be used and be effective. Our discussion in

FIGURE 3.2 Convenience, Trust, and Expertise Triangle 1.

FIGURE 3.3 Convenience, Trust, and Expertise Triangle 2.

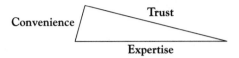

Chapters Four, Five, and Six of how to achieve these twin goals looks at what is necessary to do in order to enhance the levels of convenience, trust, and expertise at different points in the ODR process. The remainder of this chapter takes a closer look at what is included in each of these.

Convenience

In the category of convenience we include any logistical and financial factors that positively or negatively affect access to and participation in the process. What forces are present that affect the disputant's assessment of whether to begin or participate in the process? In the IRS example, a threshold level of convenience, trust, and expertise was probably met by both mail and phone. For us, talking on the phone would probably be more convenient than writing a letter, but for others the opposite might be true. Interestingly, the IRS did not suggest going to the local IRS office, something we might agree is less convenient than phone or mail. Yet, for some individuals, other factors, for example, in the context of a letter from the IRS, might be more important than convenience, and going down to an IRS office might be the option selected. As discussed in the next chapter, however, the goal of an ODR system will often be not to provide the highest possible level of convenience. Here, the IRS probably does not want people appearing at its offices when other choices better meet the agency's own personnel and budgetary needs.

Would an online option have been more convenient or less convenient than those offered? Many might prefer an online option and find it highly convenient, but, of course, for those without Internet access at all, it would not meet any threshold convenience level. For those with a very slow Internet connection the measure of convenience would be lower than for those with a high-speed Internet connection. We are currently in a transition period in which an online option may be highly convenient to someone with experience online and be highly inconvenient to the less experienced. For disputes occurring offline, therefore, ODR will not be the exclusive option until a much larger percentage of the population has easy and fast Internet access.

For those companies or institutions considering an ODR option, the challenge of convenience is complicated by the fact that the threshold level must be set at the level of the capabilities of the participant who is least able or willing to participate. If the third party and one disputant are highly sophisticated users but the other disputant is relatively new to the Internet, the convenience level must be set at the lowest common denominator unless that disputant is willing for some reason to work to raise his or her skill level. The reason for this is that there should not be a power imbalance between the parties, and technological skill and equipment that affects ability to participate can create a power imbalance.

There is no mathematical formula for measuring convenience when designing an online system. In addition to being affected by the equipment and skills required to participate, costs and other factors related to who the individual is will be important. In many contexts, individuals may be willing to sacrifice some convenience for a higher level of trust or expertise, or accept less of one of these factors in exchange for a higher level of convenience. What is needed by any system designer, therefore, is an understanding of the user base, because at every step in the online process, the participants are evaluating the process, finding it convenient or not, trustworthy or not, and of value or not. Convenient systems that are not trustworthy will not be used, nor will trustworthy systems that are not convenient be used. The system need not be the most convenient of all possible systems, but it must be convenient enough so that the value provided justifies the effort made to use it.

When Parties Have Different Degrees of Access

The problem of power and different levels of access arose in the very first case we handled after the Online Ombuds Office was established. We received the following email one day from a person we shall call Robert Gray.

> Hello . . .
>
> I am a computer hobbist, and found a void that I thought that I could fill on the net. I am from Hampshire County, Kansas and decided to publish the news from the area. I come home from work . . . read the paper, listen to the radio and watch the local television newscast and with all that . . . summarize the dailey news and events and publish this on the web at: http://. . . . . . .
>
> A few weeks ago, I was contacted by the local print media that I am in violation of copyright infringement and that I must stop immeadiatly . . . they also accused me of making money through this . . . which I don't.
>
> heard different opinions from the right to fair comment to *%#@ them!
>
> What I have done . . . . . while awaiting what my next move will be is to chop up the news even more . . . . it's like a third grader wrote it. I have many different people who have wrote in support of what I am doing. BTW . . . they also said that I was pre-empting a business oppertunity, which I feel is the real reason they want me to quite. The have an e-mail address, but DO NOT have a web site!
>
> Thank You . . .

In case it is not clear, what Mr. Gray was doing was summarizing stories from the local newspaper and placing them on a Web site he had created for the community. The newspaper had sent him several letters suggesting that he was violating the copyright laws.

A lesson that we learned very quickly from this case was that power imbalances on the Web may be different from what they would be if the parties were interacting offline. In the offline environment, Mr. Gray probably would have been no match for the newspaper. He had far fewer financial resources and, if spelling and grammar matter at all or suggest some level of sophistication, he would have been at a disadvantage.

In the context of this dispute, the tables were turned. Mr. Gray was comfortable in the online environment. He was online often and responded quickly to messages, and he could, even if his grammar and spelling left something to be desired, express his thoughts quite clearly and with emotion. We persuaded the editor of the newspaper to participate with us, but she had problems. During the Summer of 1996 when this happened, the newspaper did not have a Web site and she had poor Internet access. She had email, but to go to Mr. Gray's Web site and look at what he was doing, something she had never done, took considerable effort for her. Ultimately, we were able to successfully mediate this dispute. We did so through a multimedia approach. Using telephone, fax, and email, the newspaper quickly withdrew its objections to Mr. Gray's Web site and he agreed to file no further complaints.[1]

The Issue of Record Keeping

In addition to the problem of one party in the "Robert Gray" case being relatively unfamiliar and uncomfortable in the online environment, various participants were on vacation during different parts of the summer. We therefore decided to employ the telephone in addition to email. We believed then, and still believe, that the primary goal of any dispute resolution system must be to resolve the dispute, and the means employed should be the most appropriate means available. For some today, participating in a phone conversation may be less convenient than responding to email but that was not true for the newspaper editor.

We generally support the use of communication forums that allow one to respond at one's convenience. We thus prefer asynchronous communication options, such as email and Web-based conferencing, to chat rooms where everyone must participate at the same time. However, there should not be rigid rules about this but rather a policy that allows the third party to select among appropriate options. Some media may provide more opportunities to equalize power among the parties than other media and what is convenient will vary in different contexts and for different disputes.

While it may seem to many readers that the phone is quick and the most universally accessible medium, that may not be a correct assumption. From March to December 2000, SquareTrade handled over 30,000 disputes for a variety of online marketplaces. Disputants from over eighty countries were involved. They were in different time zones and often with different language capabilities. When the Web, in some way, breaks down language barriers and time zone differences, it becomes a decidedly more convenient forum.

One of the significant benefits of ODR is that a record is kept of all exchanges. This has consequences that we will discuss later for building feedback and intelligence into the ODR process. It also has benefits in recreating who said what, what was said, and under what circumstances. For us, and for other mediators or dispute resolution providers, the transcripts allow us to study what occurred, what decisions were made, what seems to have been handled well, and where there are possibilities for improvement. In the Web site developer and newspaper dispute, we placed the entire transcript on the Web so that others might understand the process that occurred.[2] As the transcript suggests, the use of the telephone accelerated the process and allowed a resolution to be reached.

There are issues of confidentiality in keeping and using transcripts and other records that we shall also examine on pp 159. When we decided to place the Gray transcript on the Web, some mediators told us that there were confidentiality problems even if we removed all identifying names. We did not accept that point of view, but there is a need to be vigilant about confidentiality because so many more extensive records are created with ODR.

We shall return to the issue of convenience when we discuss options for working with the parties, but it is clear that as more people become comfortable online, as speeds of transmission increase, and as software becomes easier to use, the convenience bar for the least capable of the disputants will rise. It is also clear, however, that convenience will always be one of the three factors since as levels of comfort with participating online increase, expectations of what disputants should be capable of doing may also increase, and software that allows more complex interactions among the participants is continually developed. As long as one party finds the ODR context less convenient or accessible than the other, the issue of convenience will need to be considered in developing ODR systems.

Trust

The great benefit of the online environment is commonly understood to lie in the area of convenience. We can send email to anyone on the planet, and we can do it from wherever we might be, whether we are on the ground or, if we have the right equipment, in the air flying somewhere. In general, whatever it is that we find to be miraculous about the online world more often than not will fall into the category we have loosely called convenience.

An elevated level of convenience is present in almost everything we do online. Indeed, we are typically online because what we wish to do is more conveniently done online than in some other manner. When the Net works quickly and efficiently, we seem almost to be able to ignore the laws of physics and to overcome the usual constraints of time and space.

When one is online, the absence of convenience is generally immediately apparent. Indeed, toleration of inconvenience online is so low that a frustrating experience at a Web site will probably be one's last experience there. If you are setting up a Web site, therefore, you will not need to be reminded to test how well it works and what users find clear or confusing. Means for enhancing convenience will almost always be part of any upgrade or revision. In perhaps the most notable example of the value of convenience, Amazon.com sued Barnes and Noble in late 1999 over Barnes and Noble's use of a "one click" ordering system. The fight was over the competitive advantage that was perceived to be achieved by reducing, by one or two, the number of clicks needed to order a book.

Trust is in a very different realm from convenience. We believe, frankly, that trust is as important for the success of any Web-based enterprise as convenience, but we also recognize that it is easily ignored and neglected. While lack of convenience creates a feeling of frustration, lack of trust results in a feeling of risk. With convenience, the question is whether it is easy enough to do something. With trust, one can do something but one may not want to do it because of concern that what one wants is not what one will get.

Trust is something that may be irrelevant if a user finds it difficult to negotiate a site. But trust becomes highly relevant when there is convenience and a user feels able to conduct a transaction on the site. At this point, a whole set of questions will surface, all of which contribute to how much risk a user feels in using the site. The user may, for example, ask some of the following questions:

- What are the consequences of a transaction that does not succeed?
- Is a great deal of money at stake or a small amount?
- Is one's reputation at stake?
- Is the benefit of using a new vendor or obtaining a lower price sufficient enough to take the risk of having one's judgment challenged if something goes wrong?
- Is what I am obtaining of the same quality as something that I could obtain elsewhere?
- Am I being treated fairly and the same as other users?
- Does the other party have an advantage of any kind?

At some point prior to the completion of an online transaction, cost, convenience, and the value of what is being offered will be balanced against whatever risks the user feels are present. In any E-commerce context, if you wish someone or some institution to use your product or conduct business with you, you must ask why they should change their habits and do something differently from the way they have done it in the past. There is always a cost to doing something in a new way, and this cost will involve risk of some sort. There is also a payoff that can come with doing something in a new way but whether the payoff is larger than the risk will be a question that always surfaces at some point.

Consider ClicknSettle, CyberSettle, or some other blind bidding venture. These processes are only usable when there is a single issue over which the parties disagree and that issue is quantifiable, such as money. Advocates of such processes argue that when money is the issue there is nothing to lose, because if there is no agreement, no party will be any worse off than if the process had not been used. In spite of this, "engagement rates," the rates at which second parties agree to participate, tend to be less than 50 percent. Why aren't they higher?

Blind bidding companies do understand that parties must have trust that confidential information will not be revealed to the other side. Therefore, they have all put measures in place to make their sites highly secure. But that does not seem to be enough. Nor is it enough that these sites are easy to use and certainly meet all measures of convenience. What is instructive here is that there is simply risk in doing something new. It may be that authorization from the company is needed to depart from traditional practice. There may be a need to file some forms to explain to the company that one is doing something differently from colleagues who are handling claims in the traditional manner. Whether or not the cause of the engagement rate is one of these factors or something else, any company offering a new service needs to anticipate that there will be some risk to whoever is willing to try something new.

The Trustworthiness of the Internet

The issue of trust is often ignored and also underestimated. When it is recognized, it is often assumed that it is a factor that cannot really be controlled. It is often said, for example, that there are inherent problems on the Internet involving identity and location. That is, one can never be certain whom one is transacting business with or where they are located. The famous cartoon, which has a dog in front of a computer sending a message that "on the Internet, no one knows that you are a dog," reinforces this belief.

It is true that the Internet is not inherently trustworthy. But no environment, physical or virtual, is inherently trustworthy. What is true is that in the physical world we each have experience in evaluating what level of trust is present. We also understand implicitly what should be done to raise the level of trust before we take some action. When we purchase a used car, for example, we may know who we are buying it from but we still take it for a test drive and, before making a final decision, have it examined by a mechanic.

More important than whether the Internet is inherently trustworthy or not is the question of how to make it more trustworthy. It is certainly not true that there is nothing one can do to build trust. Indeed, we shall explain that making ODR available is a rather easy trust-building action. What is fair to say is that the Internet is an environment where the usual cues we rely on to confirm identity are not present. And, of course, where someone is located will be a challenge in any situation where the party is not encountering you face to face. But all this really means is that either new cues are needed, or techniques are needed that provide the same level of trust that our usual cues provide.

An Example of Trust

Before we began our online mediation with eBay, we decided that we needed to have some sense of the eBay environment and of the experience level of users. One of our sons had been asking for a piece of software, and we decided to look and see whether anyone was offering the software for sale. It turned out that the software, which a mail order catalogue was selling for thirty dollars, was indeed being offered for sale on eBay and the current bid was only ten dollars.

We did not win the first auction but we won the second and ended up purchasing the software for fifteen dollars. The seller did not accept credit cards, so we sent him a check. We had checked his reputation on eBay using the eBay feedback rating system and were fairly confident that we would receive what we had paid for. But the child, who was used to paying for an item at a store and then immediately walking out with it, became more anxious about this purchase every day as the mail arrived without the software. For the adult, it was clear that some patience was required, that this was a different environment from face-to-face purchases, that the dollar amount that might be lost was not significant, and that the seller had a good reputation. The eBay system for creating trust worked fairly well for the adult. But this was an environment the child had no experience with, and eBay's trust-building process had much less of an impact.

All in all, for someone with little experience online, the level of trust diminished every day until the item did arrive a week later. Ultimately, the child was gratified by this experience, but he was delayed gratification and was peppered with significant frustration, as well.

What was also clear from the child's behavior was that if there had been a dispute, for this child there would have been nothing more natural than clicking on a link to an online dispute resolution resource. It also seemed to us that if the seller had a relationship with an ODR provider, the child would have been less anxious each day and perhaps also less willing to assume that we were being defrauded.

Would it matter if the ODR resource were a human or a machine? Probably not. What was clear to us was that the future will bring not only new technological resources but also individuals who will be increasingly comfortable with these resources. They will look to the online world first to provide many different kinds of needs, and there is no reason at all for them not to find effective and accessible dispute resolution services there, as well.

Knowing who one is interacting with online and where they are located are only two of many variables that can affect levels of trust. What is really being sought is a relationship that will meet expectations and avoid any later conflicts. In any transaction, one wants to be confident that what is purchased is being represented accurately, what is being promised will be delivered, that if there are explicit guarantees they will be carried out, and if there are no explicit guarantees, the other party will act reasonably.

The best builder of trust is a prior transaction that has gone smoothly. But on the Net we are often enticed by high levels of convenience or low prices that are offered by entities we do not have prior experience with. For an E-commerce site or, indeed, any site on the Web that has no brand name or well-known reputation, a stated commitment to use ODR and placing a link on the site to an ODR provider is a clear trust-building option. And it is an option that is easier to do online than it is offline.

Building trust online involves providing information to customers that tells them something about the party they are dealing with. The value of a seal or trustmark, such as those offered by SquareTrade.com, the Better Business Bureau, or WebAssured, is that a third party is providing information about the Web site owner. The Web site owner is not simply saying that he will participate in ODR if a problem arises but that he has a formal agreement with a third party to do so. Trust comes, therefore, from information on the third party's site and the reputation of the third party.

We have looked at many E-commerce sites and online marketplaces and have been surprised at how many sites assume that making a desired product easily available at a good price is all that is necessary to generate revenue. It is common for information to be provided about where funding has come from for the company, about how the company has been mentioned in the press, and what the credentials of company officials are. This information is informative, but it should not be assumed to substitute for the kind of information described above.

Online dispute resolution, we expect, will become a trust-building enhancement to many sites. It is a particularly valuable resource for building trust since ODR itself is a service that must in some way persuade potential users that it can be trusted. E-commerce sites need to build trust to increase business. ODR sites need to build trust to have a business. It is no surprise that the logo for SquareTrade includes the phrase "Building Trust in Transactions," or that eResolution uses the phrase "Integrity Online," or that WebAssured claims that it is "the dot confidence company."

In traditional mediation and arbitration, taking some action to build trust is usually at the top of the mediator's or arbitrator's agenda when the parties first meet. Traditional ADR recognizes that parties have not necessarily completely committed themselves to either the mediation process or the particular mediator, and a goal of a first meeting is both to present information about the process and also to create an environment that will support a decision to continue.

Building trust in an ODR process should be a key concern in the design of the Web site. Potential users of ODR will begin making judgments about the value of the service the first time they see the opening screen of the ODR site. There is a challenge, therefore, that is not present in face-to-face dispute resolution, since more effort needs to go into anticipating questions and concerns that users might have. There are also, however, opportunities that are not present in offline processes. There are options at an ODR site, for example, for quickly modifying information and keeping it up-to-date. An often asked question will concern the difference between mediation and arbitration, and the Web provides opportunities to do this with color and graphics, as well as with words.

We often see attempts to build trust by presenting information about how much benefit can be gained from using the site, how the site has been successfully used in the past, and how successful the founders or managers of the site are. Such information is really data about expertise, which is something we shall discuss in the next section. This is useful information to give to users, but it confuses trust with expertise. Expertise concerns whether the site has the resources and skills to successfully resolve the problem. Trust is about whether what is being promised will be delivered and about whether or not what the site is saying about itself and its expertise can be believed.

Expertise

The Net is an ever-growing, indeed infinitely expandable, information and knowledge space. It is increasingly easy to deliver information to anyone and to any place from anyone in any other place. Delivering useful, valuable, and expert information, however, is not the same as delivering expertise. Sometimes, we recognize, information alone may be sufficient to fulfill what a user needs, and easy, cheap access to information is what the Net excels at. Often, however, something more than information is required. In this sense, expertise requires an interactive informational process, one where the Web site receives information from a user, processes it in some way, provides some analysis and results to the user, and perhaps then begins the process again.

Consider the situation of a subscriber to an Internet Service Provider (ISP), who has her account canceled because it was determined that she had allowed others to use her account in ways that violated the ISP's terms and conditions. Anyone in this or any similar situation would want to know whether the subscriber has any rights and, if so, whether there are any legal remedies. In addition, the user might find online a list of persons who had experience in dealing with such problems. There might even be all sorts of information online about strategies that have proven successful in the past when dealing with that type of problem. This is all information of value and if the information has come from the Web site of an ODR provider, the sense that the ODR provider has knowledge and expertise will be enhanced.

The principle challenge of expertise, however, goes beyond providing useful information. Expertise is delivered as part of a process, which can be a one-on-one process like an interview, or a more complex process like mediation. In an online mediation, information would certainly be provided to the parties as part of the process, but the parties will find value in the process only if the mediator does something more. The mediator needs to respond appropriately to communications, to keep the parties "talking," and to move them somehow toward a mutually acceptable solution.

How Cyberspace Creates Process Options

Cyberspace is increasingly a place where there are *processes* available to users as well as *information*. This should not be surprising since processes are sets of informational transactions and exchanges. What makes building processes out of informational transactions difficult is structuring and regulating the flow of information and the numerous informational exchanges among the parties. Fighting online, negotiating online, and mediating online all involve the sending and exchanging of messages, but it is the third party's management of and involvement in the message-exchanging process that provides the value the parties are seeking.

Some processes require richer and more flexible means for managing the flow of information, and these processes are inevitably more difficult to build in the online environment. Face-to-face sessions are prized not because the parties can see each other's faces but because seeing faces adds new opportunities for communicating information and interacting efficiently. The ongoing goal for ODR programs is to gradually increase the richness of interaction online and thus allow for expertise to be applied more efficiently and effectively.

Part of the strategy for applying expertise online is to enhance those stages where the traditional model is weak. The traditional

ADR model focuses the delivery of expertise on the face-to-face sessions. The blind bidding process illustrates that there are opportunities to do some things better online than are done offline.

James Melamed describes the mediator as someone who is an educator, communication facilitator, convenor, translator, questioner and clarifier, process advisor, devil's advocate, catalyst, and detail person.[3] What can the online mediator or ODR provider do to enable the third party to perform these roles effectively? If the online environment does not allow for as interactive an environment as the offline environment, can it structure the process in a different way so as to deliver expertise to the parties? Most particularly, how can potential users be persuaded that expertise can actually be provided to them?

While many people focus on the weaknesses of the online environment, much of our thinking has gone into identifying the strengths of the Internet and how these strengths might be exploited in ways that are not possible at all offline. The Internet is an extraordinary achievement and the challenge, as we see it, is not to use the Internet to duplicate the offline dispute resolution environment but to expand our thinking and look for ways that dispute resolution expertise can be of value online. For users considering whether or not to use an ODR process, it will be information about the success of a site in doing this that will, along with convenience and trust, allow the user to construct an image of the convenience, trust, and expertise triangle and see whether it is a shape that meets the needs of the user.

We agree with the authors who wrote recently that the Internet is "the biggest collective expert known to humanity."[4] In some of the online mediations we have done, we have been more willing than we might have been offline to have comediators, or to link a mediator with a particular kind of experience with someone who has a different kind of experience. The availability of doing this increases not only because of the ease of communication but because the pool of possible mediators is not limited by geographical location.

How can we build on the existing strengths and capabilities of the Internet? The following chapters confront this challenge more directly. We think it is necessary to focus not only on what might be required of the third party human but also on something we shall label "the fourth party." This fourth party, which we identify in more detail in the next chapter, consists of the technological resources that are available via the network. Those considering use of an ODR process will receive an enhanced impression of expertise if they not only find an experienced and trained third party but a new technological participant in the guise of a "fourth party."

4

Introducing the Fourth Party

The Critical Role of Technology

Online Complaints, *When Complaining Is Too Convenient, The Goal of an Online Complaint Process, The Challenge of Managing the Online Complaint Process, Designing Online Complaint Forms;* **Engaging the Other Side,** *Planning for Arbitration, When Arbitration is Nonbinding, Mediation.*

We have suggested that a triangle, where the three sides are labeled convenience, trust, and expertise, is a useful way to visualize the qualities needed for a successful ODR process. Three is also a familiar number in traditional dispute resolution, where there are usually considered to be three parties to the process: the two disputants and the third party neutral. Even when there is a multiparty dispute with many disputants, ADR is still commonly thought to be three-sided, with all of the disputants grouped together as the two disputants and the mediator or arbitrator as the third party.

In this and the two following chapters, we propose that you think of ODR as shaped somewhat differently, as having not three parties but four, as being a square or rectangle instead of a triangle. The "fourth party," the new presence "at the table," is the technology that works with the mediator or arbitrator. Just as the role of a third party can vary in different contexts, so can the role of the fourth party. It can, in different circumstances, be more or less relied upon and be more or less influential, but the role, nature, and value of this fourth party needs to be understood and recognized.

The fourth party does not, except in a few well-defined instances such as blind bidding, *replace* the third party. But it can be considered to *displace* the third party in the sense that new skills, knowledge, and strategies may be needed by the third party. It may not be coequal in influence to the third party neutral, but it can be an ally, collaborator, and partner. It can assume responsibilities for various communications with the parties, and the manner in which the third and fourth parties interact with each other will affect many parts of the dispute resolution process.

This chapter focuses on the beginning of the ODR process. The first part of the chapter examines the very beginning stage of the ODR process: the filing of a complaint. While a common complaint form on paper is simply a device for communicating information about the problem, the electronic complaint can, and should be, something more. We consider a complaint form to be a first interaction between the participants and the dispute resolution provider, and every such interaction should be an opportunity to promote convenience, build trust, and deliver expertise. The complaint is also a beginning to the conversation that will last until there is a settlement, and the manner in which it is handled can affect much that happens later. How this part of the process is structured is particularly important for mediation where participants must perceive a serious and effective process or they may decide to leave the proceedings.

The second part of this chapter moves our attention from the complainant to the respondent and addresses the challenge of engaging the other side and securing agreement to participate in the process. This is a crucial activity because there will not be mediation or arbitration unless the second party is willing to participate. In the IRS example in the last chapter, getting both parties to the table was not a concern because the citizen was not likely to ignore the notice. Getting both parties to agree to participate will also not be a problem when there has been an arbitration clause and an agreement made prior to the transaction to arbitrate any problems. In many disputes, however, persuading the second party to participate in ODR will be a significant challenge.

Online Complaints

There are many problems that one encounters in daily life that one does nothing about. One may feel that the chances of success are low, or that the effort to prevail will be too high. It may be that the cost to resolve the dispute would be greater than the value of the dispute itself or that the time one would need to devote to resolving the dispute would be better spent in some other activity. These decisions are made so often, so routinely, and so quickly that we may not even be fully aware of the calculations as to cost and benefit.

Logistical and financial factors that affect one's participation in any dispute resolution system fall into the category we have labeled "convenience." Sometimes, even when it is highly inconvenient, we do press on and try to resolve a grievance. On the other hand, sometimes access to a dispute resolution process is quite convenient but, as noted above, we still might have reasons for not pursuing a claim. Convenience may not be the deciding factor in all such calculations, but it will be a factor. No system will be used if some threshold level of convenience is not met.

In traditional ADR systems, the key inconvenience is showing up at a particular time and place for mediation and arbitration sessions. Time and place may be mutually agreed upon, but convening all participants is never simple, and it is almost always necessary for at least some of the parties to have to rearrange other commitments. If the parties have to be brought together several times, that will only increase inconvenience. What is different about online systems is that there are more opportunities for managing convenience. Convenience in the online environment, like many other things online, is not something fixed or preordained but rather something that system designers have considerable control over.

As a simple example, forms can be designed that are either inviting and easy to fill out or intimidating and frustrating.

There are, even in the online environment, various forces that can reduce access, such as the need for special technological skills or equipment. But even such obstacles can be responded to by the system designer and minimized if desired. The network removes, or at least reduces, the inconvenience of physical place and, if software designers choose to let the participants communicate with each other asynchronously, disputants can read and submit messages whenever they wish, thus removing the inconvenience of time.

As a general rule, we would suggest that you make all parts of any dispute resolution process as easy and as convenient as possible. The main exception to this rule involves complaint forms. How easy or how hard it is to file a complaint can be regulated and, as we discuss in the next section, there are some circumstances when less than optimal access should be considered.

When Complaining Is Too Convenient

A significant attraction of ODR is how convenient it is. It is available to parties in different locations who would otherwise have no dispute resolution options. For others, access with a click of the mouse will require less time than going to a physical location to file something. Online access which is available twenty-four hours a day should be more accessible than an office that is only open from nine to five. Convenience in pursuing a complaint offline can be made more convenient if one hires a lawyer to attend to it, but then cost rises. It should not be controversial to assume that on virtually any measure of cost and convenience, the online has advantages over the offline.

Online complaint forms are not only convenient to users, but, in one sense at least, they are convenient to those who will be receiving and working with the complaints. What we mean by this is that complaint forms are relatively easy to place online. There are many instances in which there is no desire to have a whole ODR process, and there may even be no clear understanding of what options exist for an ODR process. Having an online complaint form, however, is understandable to anyone and a simple complaint form, at least, is fairly easy to add to a Web site.

Before you do place a complaint form on your Web site, thus allowing complaints to be filed anytime from anywhere and at low cost, you should consider at least one consequence of doing this: Ease of access may lead to an increase in the number of complaints being filed. If there is some trust in the system and some belief in its value and effectiveness, a low cost and easily accessible system will probably be used much more than the system it is replacing. Many people who might not have filed complaints because they couldn't be bothered getting the form and filling it out can now get it with a few clicks of a mouse and even receive some online help in filling it out.

When we did our pilot project with eBay, we received one hundred and fifty complaints over a two-week period about problems arising out of auction transactions. To our surprise, we also received about seventy-five other complaints. These complaints involved a wide variety of problems that persons who filled out our form had. There were complaints about landlords, about car dealers, about spouses, about domain names, and so on. We had anticipated receiving a lot of complaints since there were about seven hundred thousand transactions a week taking place on eBay in March 1999. But we had not thought that anyone with a complaint about anything would use the complaint option.

Who was responsible for this? We originally blamed the users because they had obviously not read carefully the language about our project. We provided the language that eBay placed on their customer service page about the dispute resolution service, and it seemed to state pretty clearly that only those with auction-related problems should contact us. As time passed, however, we decided that a good part of the blame could be placed on us. We had anticipated the problem of receiving a lot of complaints but we had not anticipated that some might misread or misunderstand what we were offering to do. We had thought that clear language was all that was necessary to control who complained about what, when we should have known that we could have designed our complaint form in a way that would have restricted non-eBay complaints.

As noted above and as we shall discuss further on p. 101, there are options for making access more difficult as well as opportunities for designing a complaint form to facilitate access. On our complaint form, for example, we had a category for "other." The simplest action to at least reduce the number of non-eBay complaints would have been not to have an "other" category. There was no real need for it. We could have done other things as well, but what is most important to understand is that we did not pay enough attention to trying to anticipate how the online form would be used. When access is easy, there is a great need for thinking through how users might decide to use it. There is also a great need to devote time to anticipating "misuse" of it.

The Goal of an Online Complaint Process

If you plan to place a complaint form online, and we do encourage you to do so, you need to use all available methods to make sure that you get complaints about the types of problems you are best able to respond to. There is more at stake here than your being inconvenienced. If complaints increase to a point where you cannot quickly respond to them, you will be committing what we would consider a major sin and something that could be quite damaging to you. That is, you will not be responding to complainants quickly enough with information about why you cannot handle their problem and perhaps providing suggestions for how they might get assistance.

We shall discuss on p. 149 why, if you are communicating with parties over the network, you must regularly and frequently communicate with them. If the online complaint is used for a dispute that will be handled offline and in a traditional way, this is less necessary. But if the complainant has never met you and will not meet you, there will be more than the usual concern about whether you are attending to his problem. In our framework, this can be considered a problem of trust. Lack of contact and communication will reduce trust. Frequent communication, however, will be a trust-enhancing mechanism. There are also online tools for automating some communications and for providing information at regular intervals about what is taking place.

After you have figured out how to limit complaints to types you wish to be filed, how easy should you make it to file a complaint? Again, we might instinctively say that access should always be as convenient as possible. For some, the primary goal for placing a complaint form online will be to increase complaints, increase caseload, and, one would hope, increase revenue. This is the right approach, therefore, if there are adequate resources to respond to the complaints and meet the expectations of complainants.

When increasing the number of complaints is intended to lead to more business and more revenue, new staff can be hired to deal with an increased caseload. At the other extreme, however, are public agencies for whom a greater caseload may not lead to increased budgetary allocations.

About two years ago, we suggested to a state agency that it should have complaint forms available online that potential complainants could download. We did not make what would have appeared to them an even more radical suggestion, namely that they have a form online so that complaints could be filed electronically over the Internet. Their immediate reaction was to wonder what this would do to their backlog of cases. There had been newspaper articles documenting that some cases had been languishing in the system for several years. The agency had seen an increase in case filings in the past several years, and its primary aim was to deal with an increasing backlog with a budget that had not increased. They wanted to reduce the caseload whereas our suggestion, even though it was recognized as being in the interests of many citizens, would only make it harder for them to achieve what was then their primary goal.

We were not happy with this reaction then and every so often renew our suggestion, but we do understand their position and they are probably correct that filings would increase if the process were made less cumbersome. Indeed, rather clear evidence of the impact of electronic complaint forms on numbers of filings is available from several sources. The Better Business Bureau, for example, placed a complaint form online in 1995 and complaints have doubled since then.[1] SquareTrade has found that when links to it are added in additional pages of a site, complaints can increase by as much as 10 percent.

The Challenge of Managing the Online Complaint Process

When complaints increase as a result of access to complaint forms becoming more convenient, there will also be questions of how to interpret what the increased levels of complaints signify. Without carefully analyzing the filing rates, it will be hard to know whether complaining is higher because there are more problems, or whether the bar to complaining has been lowered enough so that those problems one would have tried to resolve alone or not tried to resolve at all are being pursued through more formal means.

The Internet makes access to almost everything easier than it is offline. Many marketplaces make it possible to transact business with parties one would never have been able to interact with before. It should not be surprising that ODR makes access to dispute resolution easier. We believe that access should be enhanced, but we also believe that it should not be made easier until complaints can be responded to efficiently. ODR can work to save money for many entities if disputes that would have been filed offline are now filed online. But if the offline cases move online and a whole series of new cases surface because the system is available, new assessments will have to be made of available resources.

ADR came into favor at least partly because of a widespread belief that access to justice via the courts was not serving the public adequately. If one wants to see a system where it is inconvenient to complain, and it is really inconvenient by design, the court system is as good an example as any. It is so inconvenient that one needs a specialist, a lawyer, to deal with the process. Defenders of the court system can cite various justifications for the complexity of the process, but no one can claim that easy access to justice is a goal of the court system. There is, of course, a legal right for aggrieved people to use the court system, but other than the guaranty of a lawyer to persons accused of crime, very little effort is made to help people use that right.

ODR can be a means to improve access to any system, but care should be taken to anticipate caseloads and to have a system that is robust enough to handle complaints that are filed. While we have tried to alert you to how easily accessible complaint forms can increase caseloads, we should also add that, as with many problems that the online environment contributes to, effective solutions can be found online. Caseloads may increase when complaint forms are placed online, but technology is also available to allow responses to be made in an efficient way. SquareTrade, which currently handles eBay-related complaints, reports that its total caseload from eBay and the other marketplaces it services was over ten thousand in January 2001. It certainly seems possible, in the language of the online environment, to "scale up" and manage significant caseloads efficiently.

Designing Online Complaint Forms

We recently received the following email (names, location, and other identifying information has been removed):

> I'm contacting you after a preliminary web search for mediation services in your area. I'm looking for advice, help and/or referral on establishing a long distance mediation process with my former wife who lives in your town regarding a disagreement we have about our 15 year old daughter who lives with her to travel and visit me in Germany. (I used to

live in Amherst and studied in the journalism department, and now I moved back to my home country.)

Obviously there are many details involved in this case but before filling the screen with information, I would greatly appreciate if you could provide me with some guidance on how to proceed.

Thank you,
Dieter Reinhardt

The Online Ombuds Office has received complaints in two ways. We sometimes receive email of this type from people who have found us and who explain, in their own language, what the nature of the problem is. More commonly, a form we have online is filled out. The form presents a user with a series of questions about the dispute, how it arose, and who is involved. It also provides a space for a statement in the person's own words of anything else the person wishes to tell us about.

We have not gone so far as to instruct persons who write emails like this one to go to our Web site and fill out our form. But we do have a very strong preference for using Web-based forms, rather than email, to complain and communicate.

1. *We can make certain that critical information is provided.* As we have already noted, the form gives us an opportunity to solicit information that we think is important. In this dispute, it may take the exchange of several emails before we get all the information we would like to have before contacting the other party. The writer says "before filling the screen with information, I would greatly appreciate if you could provide me with some guidance on how to proceed." If he had gone to the Web site and if the Web site has been properly designed, he would have been given information about the process. If he had filled out a complaint form, particularly one that had been prepared

especially for use in family disputes, we would have received information that he did not think to include in the email.

We are able to obtain information that we feel we need to know about the dispute because when we design a complaint form, we can ask questions about all those facts and issues that are of interest to us. We will, in addition, provide some space for the user to tell us what she thinks is important, and often this information is useful. We can also, however, in a very simple way, makes certain that information that is of interest to us is submitted. If a user does not answer a question or does not make a selection from among several choices, and then clicks on the SUBMIT button anyway, a message will appear on the screen indicating that we need the information in the particular box in order to proceed.

2. *The information that is provided can be used efficiently.* Once information that we need is provided to us in a form, we can use it efficiently because it is in a standardized format. A more efficient use of data is possible with a Web form than with email because information in any box that is filled out can flow automatically into a database where it can be compared with other data and processed in some way.

We view the complaint form as not simply a means to obtain information from a user but as the beginning of a conversation with the user that, one hopes, will eventually lead to resolution. When paper forms are filed, the user is often told "we will get back to you." What this means is that the conversation has ended for a period of time and that there will be some dead time while the other party is contacted. With an online form, some information can be fed back to the user instantaneously, and, even if there is not a great deal of information exchanged and even if the response is machine-based and not from a human, the feedback tells the user that the system is working and that the process can continue.

As an example, once the complaint form identifies that there is a custody problem, there is the possibility of feedback about a range of issues from success rates in the category identified, to information about how long it usually takes for settlement, to more general information that explains certain features of ODR. This is feedback that should serve not only to inform the user about process and ground rules but also to indicate to the user that you have expertise and that you can be trusted to be back in contact within a certain period of time.

We recognize that mediation places a high value on parties telling their stories in their own words and that our process may seem to place constraints on this. It may seem that although email is inefficient, it does provide a better outlet for the complainant to shape the response according to his own wishes. This may be true, but in this particular situation the complainant is also concerned about time, and much time would have been saved if appropriate forms on the Web had been used from the beginning. As just another example, consider the second email we received from him:

Dear Janet

Thanks for your reply. Here is the information you requested.

Katja (my ex-wife) has an email account and a computer at home but I understand she is not completely into it. I anticipate that she will ask if at her end she can meet with you directly. Suzi, (our daughter) is a girl of these times, she has an email account, a computer and during this last year she got hooked with chatting on-line. We had lawyers involved for a brief period of time, during the writing of the Separation Agreement. Katja was also a student of UMass at the time, had the services of a legal services office at the University to initiate the Separation Agreement process. I had the first draft read by 2 lawyers/mediators so they could address some of my concerns (I don't remember who they were now). I hope that we won't need to have lawyers involved in solving this issue. I also have some questions. When do you think that we might be able to start the mediating process?

How long would the mediation normally take? I understand that this is hard to estimate but I would like to have a general idea. The initial plan was to have Suzi travel to Germany in mid January and I need sufficient time to make all the necessary arrangements. What kind of fee structure does your mediating service have? What are methods of payment? If you use software for the online mediation, is it downloadable? Does it come on a Mac version?

Again, thank you for your time.

Consider how many questions this person is asking and how much more labor intensive the process is than if he had answers to these questions routinely provided to him as he was filling out the form. Forms can be informative as well as a means to provide information. The email process being employed here is taking up the time of the individual, but perhaps more importantly, it is taking up the time of the mediator.

This dispute has not yet been resolved and the inefficiencies that are present in the exchanges of email thus far have not been noticed by the parties. For them, there is a high level of convenience provided by email, and the fact that email is, in various ways, interfering with the delivery of expertise, is not apparent.

There is a considerable challenge in designing forms for particular kinds of disputes. Forms are a means for obtaining information efficiently, and doing it right itself requires expertise. We are not suggesting that anyone interested in having a complaint form online needs this kind of expertise and needs to draft their own form. On the contrary, the need for such forms will create a market opportunity. Online mediators will be able to select online forms the way many offline forms are obtained from publishers. Unlike forms in print, such forms could be easily customized and even modified. For those who have no desire to do anything technical, processing the forms will be done by an outside commercial entity which is able to provide high levels of security and confidentiality.

Engaging the Other Side

If a complainant has filled out a complaint form, the respondent has to be notified and persuaded to participate. There are, at this point, considerable differences between online mediation and online arbitration and between those forms of ODR that are exclusively online and those that supplement a traditional offline ADR process. In general, where ODR is a supplement to ADR, and where face-to-face meetings are envisioned, persuading the second party to participate will likely be handled offline in traditional ways. The focus in this section, therefore, is on arbitration and mediation where a complaint has been filed online and where, in all likelihood, the dispute has arisen out of some online activity.

Planning for Arbitration

The inherent difference between arbitration and mediation, namely that parties agree to abide by the decision of an arbitrator, leads to very different challenges in trying to secure the participation of the other party. In mediation, the effort to persuade the second party to participate will generally be made after the complaint is filed. For arbitration to be effective, however, some agreement to participate will need to have been agreed to at some earlier point in time. Persuading a respondent to participate in arbitration after the complaint has been filed, it will be seen below, is unlikely to be successful.

One of the first ODR projects, the Virtual Magistrate project that was described in Chapter Two, was set up as an online arbitration project. The goal was to provide a quick and final disposition of disputes involving subscribers and their Internet Service Providers (ISP). There was a need for a process to deal with such disputes, and particularly because the focus was on a resolution within seventy-two hours, arbitration seemed an appropriate choice. Each party would submit its arguments and any evidence it might have, and a "virtual magistrate" would render a decision. The project was planned with some involvement of America Online, the largest ISP, and there were some informal understandings that AOL would direct disputes to the Virtual Magistrate project.

At some point, AOL recognized that by agreeing to allow the Virtual Magistrate to arbitrate disputes between the company and subscribers, it was allowing an arbitrator to decide disputes that it had complete authority to decide. All AOL subscribers had agreed, when they became subscribers, to a long set of terms and conditions that gave AOL the authority to terminate service for almost any reason. In one recent year, AOL had used this authority to remove more than forty thousand subscribers. Why should it agree to abide by the decision of an arbitrator in such cases?

The Virtual Magistrate project did not obtain referrals from AOL and did not succeed in persuading other ISPs to participate with it. Complainants are often involved in disputes with parties with whom there is a contractual relationship. In many such situations, such as that between subscribers and an ISP, there is an imbalance of power with one party able to exercise power unilaterally. In such situations, it is highly unlikely that the more powerful party will agree to arbitration.

We often receive messages from consumers in which they state a desire to use arbitration, rather than mediation, to resolve their dispute. They like the idea of a process where there will always be a decision and where it will be a decision that the losing party is required to carry out. This attraction of complainants to arbitration is understandable. Yet, we believe arbitration is unlikely to be the prevalent online method for resolving disputes. Whichever party perceives itself to be in a more powerful position after a dispute has arisen will tend to resist a process in which there might be a decision that goes against their interests.

Arbitration can be planned for in advance, and, prior to any dispute occurring, both parties may be willing, as a sign of good faith or for some other reason, to agree to arbitration. For one side to offer to place an arbitration clause in an agreement can be a way to raise the level of trust. This will only occur, however, if both parties are aware that an arbitration clause is present. It is a common experience to agree to the terms of a contract by clicking an "I agree" button that appears on the screen. Such contracts are legally binding, but the presence of an arbitration clause in such an agreement, where one party may not be aware of all the terms, will lead to a lowering of the level of trust.

An example of the latter is an arbitration clause in a contract that a consumer might agree to before a purchase. There is strong public policy against the use of such arbitration agreements for consumer-merchant transactions. Almost all consumer groups oppose binding arbitration in the consumer context for several reasons. There have been many publicized instances of consumers who feel that arbitration worked against them. In addition, an agreement to arbitrate may also include an agreement not to go to court if a problem arises. Consumers may not have been aware that they were giving up their rights to sue by agreeing to arbitrate. This is important because there are situations in which the amount of damages that is possible with litigation can greatly exceed that which is possible under the arbitration agreement.

In Europe, such binding arbitration clauses in consumer contracts are not permitted, and the European approach is something that will be influential in the United States because many online transactions are cross-border transactions involving European parties. One possible way of satisfying concerns over consumers giving up rights in exchange for an agreement to arbitrate is to make the arbitration award binding only on the seller or to have a process in which there is an arbitrator but the decision is nonbinding.

When Arbitration Is Nonbinding

You might think that a process in which decisions are not binding should not really be called arbitration. Yet, nonbinding arbitration may become a popular form of ODR. It will give the parties an opportunity to test their arguments, to confront each other, and to hear a decision from a third party who favors neither side. While a loser in such a process could still go to court, it is likely that the litigation option will not be exercised very often if the losing party senses that they have obtained a fair hearing and that their position was not as persuasive as they might have thought it was.

We already have experience with nonbinding online arbitration. This is the form of arbitration employed in the thousands of disputes that have been handled through the ICANN process of domain name dispute resolution. Arbitration clauses are agreed to when a domain name is registered. If a trademark holder files a complaint with a dispute resolution provider accredited by ICANN, the respondent may lose his domain name if he does not respond. Enforcement of the arbitrator's decision occurs by the domain name registrar transferring the name, if that is what the arbitrator rules.

The ICANN arbitrations have achieved their goal of having disputes handled out of court in an expeditious manner. There were over 2500 complaints filed during the first year the policy was in effect. The ICANN process would seem to meet threshold levels of convenience and expertise. One of the providers, eResolution, uses an all-online process and there do not seem to have been problems for parties in using it. The other providers enhance convenience by using paper as well as the telephone when necessary to communicate efficiently with one of the parties or with the arbitrator. In terms of expertise, there have been some highly controversial decisions that many feel have misinterpreted or misapplied the policy, but there have probably not been enough of these to raise serious questions about the overall level of arbitrator quality.

The ICANN experience is important to us less because of the importance of the domain name issue and more because of what it tells us about building an arbitration process into any online venture. A lot of attention has focused on ICANN because it is, in a sense, a public body and a body that is exercising authority over a fundamental component of the Internet: domain names. Yet, the same questions raised about arbitration in the ICANN context can be raised about an arbitration process put forward by a completely private enterprise. Neither a private entity nor a public one will be rewarded for offering ODR if the process provided is found wanting in terms of convenience, trust, and expertise, and private bodies will suffer as well. If ODR is being provided to enhance trust in some commercial enterprise, something we believe every commercial venture can and should do, the process that is put in place needs to be seen as fair and impartial. This is easier to attain with mediation because mediation relies on agreement being reached between the parties, and parties can leave the process at any time. There is more coercion in the arbitration context and coercion will inevitably be suspect. This suspicion must be anticipated and means for answering any questions of bias or lack of fairness must be readily apparent.

ICANN was not insensitive to the issue of placing arbitration clauses in registration agreements that are probably never read. In light of this, one step it took was to use a process that was nonbinding. The decisions, unlike traditional arbitration decisions, cannot be enforced in court. To the contrary, the loser can go to court and start anew. Nonbinding arbitration may seem to some to remove the defining essence of arbitration, but it is a procedure that will probably be used often in many different contexts. It gives the disputants an opportunity to present their arguments in front of a neutral third party. If the parties are satisfied with the quality of the third party (expertise) and believe that they received a fair hearing (trust), they often will not take the case to court even when the arbitrator has ruled against them.

ICANN also did a few other things to try to achieve a perception of fairness and raise the level of trust. To allay suspicions that one dispute resolution provider was being favored, it decided that it would authorize several dispute resolution firms to decide domain name disputes. As of late 2000, there were four such firms, and more may be added. It also allowed respondents who were dissatisfied with the arbitrator selected to ask for a three-person panel and to participate in the selection of the other panel members.

In spite of these precautions, ICANN made one highly flawed decision that has lowered levels of trust and has begun to raise very serious questions about the legitimacy of the whole process. They decided to allow the complainant in a domain name dispute to choose the arbitration provider. We shall not go into great detail in analyzing the problem ICANN faces because it is really not necessary to do so to see why allowing the complainant to choose the provider, at least in this context, was a decision that could lower the trust level below a threshold level. Simply consider the following chart—Figure 4.1, which shows the percentage of cases that the three largest providers have. The one with the highest percentage is the World Intellectual Property Organization, and their percentage seems to be increasing over time. Why would this occur?

One plausible answer is that prospective complainants are aware that the World Intellectual Property Organization (WIPO) finds for the complainant over 80 percent of the time. The provider with the fewest number of cases, eResolution, has arbitrators who find for the complainant less than 60 percent of the time. If you were filing a complaint over a domain name, which provider would you choose? If you saw these differences in how the providers were

FIGURE 4.1 Number of UDRP Complaints Filed per Provider Each Month (January 2000–January 2001).

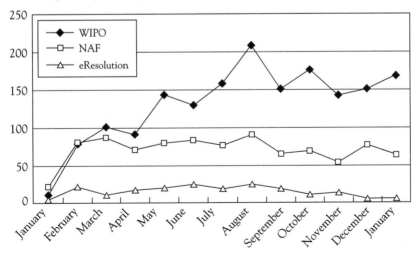

ruling and also saw that complainants are still allowed to select the provider, how legitimate would the process seem to you?

We believe that it is generally bad policy to build an arbitration agreement into a list of terms and conditions that, in all likelihood, the user has not read. This is less of a problem in an arbitration agreement that the seller has agreed to be bound by but the buyer is not bound by. Such an agreement can, indeed, be trust-enhancing. However, a nonbinding arbitration clause such as ICANN has, in which the loser can go to court, may turn out to be quite the opposite of trust enhancement if the only losers who go to court are complainants, namely trademark holders. Because courts are highly inaccessible because of their cost, the option of going to court may be illusory for many domain name holders.

It will be interesting to see whether ICANN realizes that its own legitimacy can be damaged if its dispute resolution process is perceived to be unfair. The main lesson from this noteworthy and ongoing experiment in online arbitration is that the first version of any system, like the first version of any computer program, will need to be revised after patterns of use have been observed. It will generally be beneficial to have a dispute resolution process that is quicker and less costly than litigation. Any system that is put in place, however, should also generate data that can be used to evaluate whether planned-for levels of convenience, trust, and expertise are being met.

Mediation

If you are angry and feel that you have been wronged, it is quite understandable that you would want a process like arbitration. Arbitration satisfies a variety of concerns:

- It will have a clear and final result.
- It will be fairly quick.
- It is understandable to most people since the arbitrator resembles, in many ways, a judge.

As we noted earlier, however, in the absence of an arbitration agreement, we would expect that mediation, rather than arbitration, would be the more commonly available dispute resolution process on the Internet. There are many qualities of mediation that have made it a popular and useful process, but it is really one quality that will lead to its wide use online. That is, participation in mediation involves little risk and, therefore, engaging the other side will generally be easier. The desire for arbitration really means that one of the parties views the process as possessing high value and low risk. The problem is that the other party is likely to view arbitration as possessing low value and high risk. Mediation offers something to both sides. Risk is reduced because both sides must agree upon any resolution and because either party can leave at any time. Mediation, in other words, may meet threshold levels of all three factors for both sides more often than arbitration would.

In situations where there is an arbitration agreement and the respondent has agreed in advance to participate in arbitration, it may still be desirable to suggest that the parties try a consensual process like mediation first. If an agreement is not forthcoming, arbitration can still be employed. Although a guarantee of resolution will not be present with the mediation alternative, there are several features of mediation that may be attractive to the parties, and there is little to lose. The benefits of mediation include the following:

- *Flexibility*—Mediation allows the parties to craft a solution that meets the parties' particular needs.

- *Relationships*—Mediation may be less adversarial, less likely to add to hostile feelings, and more likely to find a solution that will preserve a relationship and allow the parties to work together in the future.

- *Enforcement*—Mediation requires the parties to agree to a resolution. When the parties buy into a solution, rather than have it imposed on them, there are less likely to be significant enforcement problems.

We noted earlier that anyone who encounters a problem or dispute will quickly and routinely make a calculation to decide whether to pursue some further action or not. When a respondent is asked to participate in mediation, there will also be a calculation about whether to agree to participate. This is a critical calculation since the respondent can just as easily refuse to participate as agree to participate. When we first established the Online Ombuds Office and started receiving cases, we often indicated to respondents that they had nothing to lose by participating with us and that they risked nothing. If they wished to leave at any point, they were free to do so.

The value of mediation is that it is not coercive. It can also be said that the problem with mediation is that it is not coercive. We were certainly more successful in attracting cases than the Virtual Magistrate, but we were also often not able to persuade all respondents to participate with us. We were a university-based and foundation-funded project, and we used these signs of impartiality and expertise to persuade respondents to work with us. Gradually, however, we began to understand that it was not sufficient to simply say "give us a try." Rather, we had to offer something positive to the respondents or point out some benefit that could come to them by participating.

When we began our eBay project, we assumed that about half the respondents would agree to work with us. The aspect of the project that surprised us more than anything else was that almost 80 percent of respondents were willing to engage in mediation. Why would most eBay users be willing to participate with us? Whether or not they actually wished to reach a mutually acceptable outcome, they typically had concerns about further participation and involvement in eBay and about how the dispute might affect their future in eBay. eBay was important to them and eBay ran its site in such a way that a user's eBay future could be affected by disputes that arose. If they ignored us, they did so at some risk to their future online life and even to their economic well-being.[2]

For these respondents, there was risk if they did not participate. eBay advertises itself as a "personal trading community," and it is indeed a kind of community in that there are pressures on members to work to keep problems at a minimum. These pressures concern one's reputation. eBay has a process for sellers and buyers to acquire reputations as trustworthy parties. After any transaction is completed, buyers and sellers may post feedback as to the conduct of the buyer or seller. The "feedback rating" system is a software-supported reputational system, and anyone's feedback rating is accessible from the page advertising any item for sale. Checking on a seller's feedback rating is probably the first step any user takes before considering whether to bid on an item, and acquiring a positive feedback rating is thus highly important. Protecting one's feedback rating looms large in any eBay user's mind. As one guidebook to eBay points out, "on eBay, all you have is your reputation."[3]

The ideal of mediation is as a voluntary process. The underlying theory is that parties who freely and equally come to a mutually satisfactory and beneficial agreement will also be committed to carrying out the agreement. In offline mediation, however, court referrals are a high source of disputes that are mediated, and it is open to question how voluntary such mediations are. In cyberspace, we are likely to see many marketplaces adopting ODR options for participants, and while pressures arising out of the marketplace are not the same as pressures exerted by a court, it is marketplace pressures that may raise the "engagement rate" significantly.

Obtaining the participation of the respondent online has many similarities to obtaining the participation of respondents offline. What is different is that some opportunities are available to the online mediator to start building trust at this point. Respondents will have access to more information about the mediator or the mediation organization than there might be in the offline context. Data can be provided in a way that is similar to the data provided to complainants about the success rate and the average length of time needed to resolve a dispute. In the offline environment, these kinds of data are always estimates, whereas in the online world, figures and statistics can be provided.

Although the initial contact with the respondent is like the initial contact made by a case coordinator, you are also trying to get information from that party and in effect are beginning the fact-finding phase of the open session at the same time. The reason for trying to elicit information from the initial contact relates to the time factor—most of these situations will take a while to resolve, but there is usually a great deal of impatience on the part of one or both parties to resolve it as quickly as possible.

The next two chapters describe continuation of the mediation process in two different contexts. In Chapter Five, we focus on the use of ODR as a supplement to dispute resolution that is being handled traditionally and when face-to-face meetings will occur. In Chapter Six, we examine the more complicated situation in which the parties cannot meet face to face and the dispute resolution process occurs exclusively online.

5

Facilitating Agreement

ODR and Offline Dispute Resolution

Online Resources in Offline Dispute Resolution, *Employing a Web Site, Obtaining a Web Site, Using a Simple Web Site, Enhancing a Web Site, Using the Medium Strategically, A More Complex Example.*

ODR is not only a valuable resource for online activities, businesses, and dispute resolution professionals, it also offers added value to offline undertakings as well. If you are running a large or small business, for example, you might find it worthwhile to explore how your operation could be enhanced by integrating an online dispute resolution process into your business practice. ODR had its origins in disputes that were arising online and for which traditional means of dispute resolution were unavailable or inefficient.[1] There is an obvious need for ODR in the E-commerce context because there may be no alternative to the online option. Yet, the tree of ODR is likely to develop at least two branches. In addition to the obvious branch of the exclusively online process, something we shall focus on in the next chapter, there is the branch of ODR as it will be used in offline-based arbitrations and mediations.

In recent months, we have heard of plans for using ODR in employment discrimination disputes, worker's compensation disputes, and even in disputes that have begun in a state court system. We are not surprised that as media attention has been given to

ODR in E-commerce disputes, many have begun to realize that what works for online disputes can also be applied to offline disputes. Entrepreneurs and innovative mediators and arbitrators have recognized that many of the tools and resources that can help when face-to-face meetings are not possible, can help as well when they are. One of the most publicized examples of technology-facilitated dispute resolution, the blind bidding systems used for insurance claims, is the best current example of this. These blind bidding processes also illustrate that if we can identify interactions that are difficult, cumbersome, or inconvenient offline, we may be able to find online processes to improve them.

There is nothing particularly novel in suggesting that very traditional arbitrators and mediators employ a variety of modes of communication to assist parties. Offline arbitration and mediation are already multimedia processes. By this we mean that while face-to-face meetings may be considered the most important element of an offline dispute resolution process, many exchanges of information will occur via fax, telephone, and snail mail. These uses of other media are not controversial, partly because they are clearly supplementary and do not interfere with the core face-to-face encounter, and partly because they are such a familiar part of the regular array of communications tools used routinely in every office.

We suspect that email will fairly quickly join these other means of communication as something that is not exceptional and is used universally. For many people, email is already used as commonly as and even more frequently than the telephone. For others, that day will soon come.

The increasingly routine use of email was evident most recently in the Microsoft antitrust case. Before U.S. District Court Judge Thomas Penfield Jackson issued his ruling that Microsoft had violated the antitrust laws, he appointed Federal Court of Appeals judge Richard Posner to try to mediate a settlement. In late March 2000, it was reported that Judge Posner "peppered both sides with faxes, emails and phone calls about proposals and counterproposals.

The parties have not dealt face to face, but instead have been working through Posner, who has been acting in the role of an electronic shuttle diplomat."[2]

The use of email in any settlement process will, quite soon, not be a newsworthy event. When email is the only use of the network and only occasionally used, we would not even suggest that our figurative "fourth party" is present. The fourth party begins to appear as network-based tools and resources acquire a larger role, one in which the network does something more than the telephone or some other means for exchanging communication. We shall see that even something as modest as setting up a Web site for a dispute can change the dynamic of parties interacting with each other, the ways they generate options and evaluate proposals, and how they monitor enforcement.

Much of the power of mediators resides in their control over the process of communication. The richer the interaction, the more mediators can use their skills to assist the parties to move toward consensus. Mediators do this not simply by letting the parties talk but by managing the flow and exchange of information. Networks can change how mediators interact with the parties, and our approach in this chapter is to look at some specific strategies and existing resources that we believe can be employed to enhance traditional dispute resolution processes. Even if most of the process continues in offline settings, as online tools are relied on you will find a new partner, what we think of as a "fourth party," becoming part of the process.

Online Resources in Offline Dispute Resolution

Our most general principle of technology use is that one should employ the simplest technology that is appropriate for the kind of problem that needs to be resolved. We thus have no problem with the use of email for occasional exchanges, like when a clarification of something is needed, or when telephone tag is getting in the way of using the phone, and in other situations where the goal is to use a communications tool that is more efficient or convenient than telephone or fax.

Email, because it is the first online resource anyone becomes familiar with, can be considered the lowest common denominator of online tools. As noted above, if the network is only being used for occasional communications or inquiries, email will work fine. What is also true, however, is that the more email is used, the more the parties will see that it is not the perfect means for all kinds of online interactions. Indeed, and perhaps surprisingly, many of the benefits to the parties of using email will decline the more it is used. On the other hand, Web-based tools and methods of communication may be less familiar to the parties and require some getting used to. Over time, however, it will be recognized that Web-based software is not only more secure, but that it organizes communications better and also supports tasks other than the exchange of discrete messages. In other words, the more online communication that takes place, the more reliance there should be on Web-based communication tools rather than email.

Looked at from the perspective of our triangle of convenience, trust, and expertise, email should be used as long as it remains convenient and provides a sufficient level of expertise. Email is convenient, but as time passes and more and more messages are exchanged, it actually becomes less and less convenient because a burden is placed on users to manage and organize them efficiently. Web-based alternatives, on the other hand, may seem less convenient at first, but ease of use rises over time, and most importantly, tools and resources become available that would not be accessible when email is the primary vehicle for online interaction.

The next section explains how even the single act of setting up a Web site for a dispute can enhance any dispute resolution process for any kind of dispute. Creating a simple Web site for this purpose is also much less complicated than might be imagined. In subsequent sections, we explain how tools and resources can be added to the site and how this too will be something that anyone currently using the Web should look into.

Employing a Web Site

When you hear the word "server," do you first think of someone who brings you food in a restaurant? Or does the phrase "Web server" come to mind? Most likely, even if you have indeed heard of Web servers, the idea of somehow setting up a Web site as part of a dispute resolution process may seem daunting. Even if you happen to have a Web site that informs people about you and your practice, it is more probable than not that you paid someone to design it and set it up for you. Yet, we believe that even if all you feel confident doing online is looking at sites using a browser, our suggestions about employing a Web site are quite realistic.

Before we explain how one might obtain a Web site for a dispute, let's understand why doing so, even for a dispute that is being handled mostly offline, is desirable. We shall discuss later some more elaborate kinds of Web sites that an all-online arbitration or mediation might employ, but the Web site for a dispute in which there are face-to-face meetings can, in many cases, be relatively simple, inexpensive, and accessible.

A Web site is simply a space that exists online. Like a physical space, it can be large or small, artistically impressive or unimpressive, limited in function or quite powerful. How it is used, what it is used for, and what tools and resources are placed in it are decisions that the third party will be confronted with. That may raise some new questions for third parties who have handled disputes in traditional ways for a long time. It is probably inevitable that if the third party does not suggest use of the Web, at some point one of the parties will suggest it as a desirable method for doing various kinds of tasks.

The value of having a Web site for a dispute is it then becomes a single online place where any participant can go to find any information or resource related to the dispute. Although it might be tempting for a mediator or arbitrator to distribute files as email attachments, or send separate emails to all parties whenever something needs to be done, it becomes much more efficient to have a central place which can serve as a filing cabinet, scheduler, drafting table, and so on. It is also a more secure method of handling data. A single URL, or online address, is a place that all parties can have access to from anywhere at any time. It can be password-protected and made as secure as the parties wish it to be. It can be filled with resources or be a very simple space. It can have tools built into it or it can have links to tools at other sites. It will, perhaps, seem less convenient at the start than will the idea of circulating emails whenever something needs to be done. We are confident, however, that ODR is likely to be increasingly Web-oriented rather than email-oriented because ODR cannot reach its potential if simple email becomes the communications tool of choice.

In contrast to a Web site used for a dispute where the whole mediation or arbitration occurs online, the Web site we suggest be used here will not contain all the resources that will be employed in trying to reach consensus. It will not be *the* dispute resolution space. Rather, it will contain a set of tools that the parties will employ only when they seem preferable to traditional offline methods. It can, at a minimum, serve as a filing cabinet for any materials the parties wish to submit or share, but it can be a more active part of the process in ways we will describe below.

Obtaining a Web Site

Where would you start if you were involved in a dispute and wanted to do what we suggest? Many mediators and arbitrators already have Web sites that describe their expertise and experience. These tend to be static Web sites in the sense that that they display information that someone has decided all users should see. They might contain answers to frequently asked questions and even provide a link to a complaint form. One mediator we know has found it extremely useful to place his schedule of available meeting times on his Web site.[3] Such Web sites will undoubtedly be looked at when someone is considering whether to participate in a dispute resolution process with you. They may provide examples of how you use the Web or have used it. Such sites, in other words, can serve many useful informational functions and should be employed to raise levels of trust and expectations of expertise. Yet, this kind of informational site is not the kind of Web site we have in mind for assisting in a particular dispute resolution process.

The Web site that we are suggesting be set up should provide access to tools the parties can use to communicate, collaborate, and try to reach agreement. How many tools are present and how often they are used will shape how influential a role the "fourth party" will play. Before describing more specifically what these tools might do, let us suggest several different ways to set up a Web site of this kind. Even though this kind of site will be more sophisticated than a simple informational site, the means for setting it up can actually be much simpler.

1. The easiest and cheapest way is to set up a Web site of the kind offered for free by companies such as Yahoogroups.com, netunify.com, Intranets.com, eProject.com, and, WebEx.com. Links to similar sites and discussions of the relative merits of such sites can be found on the Web.[4] These sites are designed to enable members of a group to interact with each other. They provide the kinds of applications that groups need in order to function effectively. Almost all of these sites allow one to set up a site for a particular group that includes conversational capabilities, options for storing documents, group calendars, and some other useful tools like mechanisms to survey members and calculate results.

   All one needs to do to have such a Web site is to fill out a form requesting one. While these sites are password-protected, they do not provide the highest level of security, and while they are cost-free, they may include advertisements. If parties are informed of this in advance, however, such sites, because they are highly convenient, may be the best place for you to begin using the Web to enhance an offline process.

2. The free sites just mentioned are designed for use by any kind of group involved in any kind of group activity. A second alternative would be to take advantage of sites that have been designed for dispute resolution processes that are exclusively online. As ODR becomes more widely used, we can expect more resources to be designed specifically for online mediators and arbitrators. There are already sophisticated multifeatured online "spaces" for arbitration used by eResolution.ca and for mediation by SquareTrade.com, OnlineResolution.com, and others. These or other providers may offer to rent "space" to third parties or to firms that have a need for ODR. This would be a cost of doing business for a mediator that may seem unusual today but that we expect will become quite common. While such sites are probably of greatest value in arbitrations or mediations that are exclusively online, there is no reason why they cannot be employed in more complex offline interventions. Their great advantage is that they have been designed specifically for ODR and typically provide very high levels of security.

3. A third and somewhat hybrid alternative would be to have a simple Web site that has links to specific tools available for use by mediators and arbitrators. These sites would contain resources offered by companies that will not themselves resolve disputes but understand that online tools can assist in any kind of dispute resolution process. These sites, such as one planned by Agreeonline.com, would not only make tools available but would explain how the tools might be employed in particular circumstances. Eventually, for example, one might go to such sites and ask a question such as "what tools are available for a construction dispute involving a building not receiving a certificate of occupancy at the time agreed to for completion." Or, there may even be sites that could, for a fee, provide a Web site with all the appropriate tools that might be used for a construction dispute.

Using a Simple Web Site

In 1997, we were asked to advise an environmental mediation firm about what is called a "negotiated rulemaking." Under the federal Safe Water Act, many parties representing many different interests, such as local governments, corporations, and environmental lobbyists, were asked to come to an agreement about what might be acceptable levels of certain chemicals in water.

The representatives of these groups were meeting face to face every few months. In between the face-to-face meetings, the parties wanted to do something that would make the time in between meetings more productive. We were asked whether we might make available a Web site with some very simple resources, for example, a calendar, an agenda, a place to put some online documents, and a means for some discussions to take place.

These were not hard for us to do since we had special software that supported Web-based discussions and setting up a Web site where documents could be stored and accessed is among the most elementary uses of the Web. A calendar, however, was not something that we had available at the time. What was wanted was not simply a display of the days of the month or year, but an interactive calendar that permitted any participant to schedule an event or phone conversation or time frame. The participants wanted to be able to click on a date on the screen, type in the information, and have it appear on the calendar for all to see.

This did not seem as if it should be a difficult task. A calendar with boxes made from columns and rows can be drawn on paper in a few seconds. When used in a face-to-face context, anyone present can pencil in whatever information they wish in any of the boxes. We thought, therefore, that it would not be hard to find the software so that this could be done electronically by anyone from anywhere.

We ultimately did find an interactive calendar, but we also came to realize that online calendars of the type desired are artifacts that are fairly complex. In the face-to-face context, all who are present have permission, merely by their presence, to place something on the calendar. There is no control over anyone's handwriting, so the only expectation concerning appearance is that what is written be legible. And if someone in the room does write something in one of the boxes, it is also typically announced out loud so that everyone in the room becomes aware of it.

For an online calendar, some of these seemingly simple communications processes become fairly complicated. For example, before allowing someone to add something, there must be a system for authenticating a user and proving that the user has permission to modify the calendar. There are questions to be decided as to how data might best appear on the screen because we have complete control over the font and color used. Finally, there are choices to be made as to how other participants should be notified that something new has been scheduled. Should an email be sent every time a change is made? Should the parties be expected to check the Web site every day or week? Calendars may be familiar, and in the offline world, a rather simple artifact. The online versions, however, are a reminder that some things that are taken for granted in the offline environment can require considerable expertise in order to replicate online.

Interactive online calendars were hard to find in 1997, and such a calendar was a tool that we briefly attempted to develop ourselves. As it turned out, we were not the only ones to recognize that an online calendar that allowed access to members of a far-flung group was a good idea. Demand for such a product was present, and as a result, such calendars, like the other tools we were asked to provide, can today be obtained rather easily and cheaply.

The Web sites we mentioned above, such as Yahoogroups.com, netunify.com, or Intranets.com, that are intended to support working groups with members in different places, typically provide all these basic tools. They allow online discussions, provide group calendars, and make it possible for documents to be uploaded and pages of links to be created. They are also competing with each other to expand the array of tools that are offered. It is hoped this will continue because ODR is a group process involving communications and decision making. These should be usable for various dispute resolution purposes, and they should be usable with little learning required by the participants.

Such Web sites, like any online tool or resource, should be evaluated in terms of our three goals of convenience, trust, and expertise. These Web sites are not as convenient as email might be, but they should pass the threshold test of being convenient enough. They are cost-free or inexpensive, and have been designed for use by many people for many different purposes.

In terms of trust, these sites do not deliver the highest level of security. They do require passwords, and records are kept of when access has occurred and by whom. They would, we believe, meet the threshold test in the vast majority of situations, namely that they provide enough security for participants to be comfortable that only the persons for whom information is intended will have access to it.

These sites also would not rate the highest in the delivery of expertise. When used to supplement a face-to-face process, however, they are only being relied on to add to the level of expertise. For such a purpose, they should be adequate, and if there are links to additional kinds of tools and resources, the level of expertise expected will increase.

These sites provide what might be considered to be baseline ODR Web sites, providing a minimal toolset but also some very useful applications. If, for some reason, you judge that these currently free sites do not meet threshold levels of convenience, trust, or expertise, there are the other Web-based services mentioned earlier that have been designed specifically for dispute resolution.

Enhancing a Web Site

If every mediator has a toolkit of some kind, that is, a range of approaches, strategies, and skills that are employed to bring the parties to consensus, cyberspace brings the opportunity to add to that toolkit. Figure 5.1 identifies several of the tools that a "fourth party" might contribute to a dispute resolution process that is occurring primarily offline.

FIGURE 5.1 The Fourth Party.

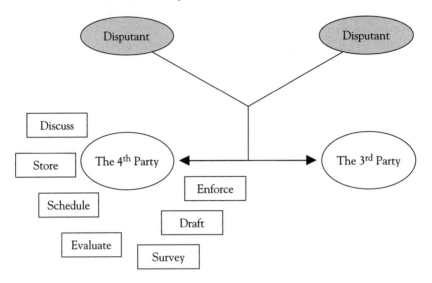

There are, as already mentioned, widely available online discussion tools that allow exchanging information, and there are tools that support the sharing of information. There is no need to pay for higher-end tools if the dispute is reasonably simple. Remember, however, that the tools should be convenient, and reasonably easy to use, and provide a threshold level of trust and expertise. If the dispute is more complex, or if the dispute is about something of considerable value, the balance of convenience, trust, and expertise may shift, and more sophisticated resources might need to be employed.

The more specialized communication needs to be, the more it is likely that the generic systems will be lacking in some way. For many arbitrations, however, a site that simply makes exchanging information and sharing documents possible may be quite adequate. For arbitration conducted completely online, as we shall discuss in the next chapter, it may be that there are actually legal questions that are more of an obstacle than technical issues.

For mediations that use the Internet to supplement face-to-face meetings, the challenge will be different than it is for mediations where the process is exclusively online. Parties who have met will use tools differently, perhaps even more effectively, because they have had a face-to-face experience. In the next chapter we shall examine various challenges that surface when a whole process is placed online. Here, the challenge is to select and employ the right tool at the right time. A sample of some of the tasks for which these tools might be employed includes the following:

1. *Blind bidding*—A simple tool that can be employed whenever there is a single sticking point and the sticking point involves money or something else that is quantifiable. There are various companies that are built around making blind bidding available under the most secure conditions. Blind bidding tools can be expected to become available that are less elaborate but that can be plugged in or experimented with whenever all issues except a single monetary issue have been resolved and when the mediator thinks it might be worthwhile to assess how far apart the parties are on some quantifiable issue.

2. *Enhanced negotiation*—Mediators should be familiar with negotiation software that might be employed in advance of or in connection with mediation sessions. Such software can assist parties in resolving the dispute, or some parts of the dispute, before calling on the services of a mediator.

   For sophisticated online users, SmartSettle (formerly called OneAccord) is very powerful software that can provide parties with alternative solutions and help parties assess what tradeoffs they are willing to make. The mediator, in such circumstances, could play a valuable role in facilitating use of the software and providing information about how it works. Alternatively, parties might employ SquareTrade's direct negotiation process that is easier to use and has proven quite effective, even though it provides no machine-based assessment of positions or proposals.

Consider, for example, how such software might be employed by credit card companies who, as a matter of policy in the United States, refund money to someone who has charged a purchase on the credit card and is dissatisfied. While the credit card companies now must look into every "charge back" claim, software that brought the disputing parties together one more time might resolve many problems. For those disputes that did not settle through negotiation, an online mediator might be employed for some of the remaining disputes.

3. *Interest identification*—A key challenge in any mediation is identifying the interests of the parties. This can be difficult because some parties may not be clear about what their priorities are. In other situations, parties try to hide their interests so as to give them more flexibility in bargaining. Interest identification in offline settings is often considered a separate stage in the process. In the online environment, interest identification can be enhanced through ongoing collection and assessment of data.

   For example, parties can be asked on the complaint and response forms what their main goals are. These questions can be asked again at later points in the process and anything listed can be ranked, or values can be assigned to further identify how important any interest is considered to be. All this collected information can be looked at to judge whether there has been any movement and whether differences have been narrowed. The blind bidding systems indicate the value that a machine can add by collecting and evaluating quantitative information. Machines can collect nonquantitative information and, if the information is standardized, make some assessments of whether or not differences exist and whether changes have occurred over time.

4. *Polling*—We already have reliable tools for asking questions, receiving responses, and displaying results. Surveys and polling can be employed to obtain information in between

face-to-face meetings. One benefit of having a Web site for a dispute is that results can be viewed there.

5. *Drafting*—For a group to sit around a table and draft a document is never an easy task, but if the document is relatively short, it will be quite manageable. There will be specific language suggested, commented upon, modified, further commented upon, and so forth. Anyone in the role of secretary will likely have paper with many items crossed out and added in. If notes are being kept on a computer, there will be a neat final version but probably no record of all the suggestions that were made and then revised.

Drafting a document online is a much more complicated task than it may seem. We have often been involved in trying to reach agreement among parties on the language in a document. This was generally done by circulating the document as an attachment to an email message. This seemed fairly cumbersome, particularly since the more changes that were made, the more drafts and attachments had to be circulated. If several circulated at about the same time, it was increasingly difficult to keep track of which was the most recent draft and what the most recent changes made were. It was not hard to come to the conclusion that there should be a better way.

We worked with Professor Patrick Wiseman of the Georgia State College of Law to develop a way to have a single text on the Web that any participant in a mediation could modify. As with much software, initial versions have been usable by sophisticated users but not average users. There is still, unfortunately, no satisfactory, simple, and accessible way to do this on the Web because creating an online "single-text" tool must allow access but not too much access, and it must allow some editing but not too much editing.

The challenge in creating a Web-based single-text tool should be obvious to anyone who has employed the "track changes" tool that is present in most word processors. When this feature is turned on, changes one makes in a document will appear in one color. If the file is sent to someone else and that person makes changes, those changes will appear in a different color. At some point, the screen becomes so cluttered with language in different colors and with words crossed out, that the machine understands who has changed what, but the human has lost the ability to do so.

6. *Monitoring enforcement*—For many transactional disputes, compensation or some other agreed-to solution may take place right away. In many other disputes, however, an agreement will be reached that requires the parties to do something in the future. Monitoring performance has never been a very efficient process. If my check has not arrived, for example, do I need to call the other party? Or should I have the mediator do it? One function of a Web site should be to monitor enforcement. If payments are required at intervals, automatic reminders can be sent. Boxes can be clicked on to indicate that a payment has been sent or some other action has been taken. Obviously, the complexity of monitoring tools will have to be appropriate to the complexity of the performance required. Certainly, however, a "legal watchman" or early warning system of nonperformance will be quite useful.

Using the Medium Strategically

The medium's visual capabilities provide intriguing possibilities for alerting us to change and indicating the direction of change. Images and numbers can be employed to show change in ways that are not possible with print. Increases and decreases can be demonstrated visually through changes in size, shape, or color. In the contract context, for example, lack of performance might send a red flag to the attorney for one of the parties. This could be an actual image of a red flag, and the red flag, if ignored, could grow larger over time, something that would be both meaningful and attention getting.

Mediators place great faith in interpreting and responding to the spoken word. At a distance, text is assumed to be the primary mode of communication. One of the more deep-rooted effects of the online environment, however, may lie in its support of visual communication. ODR, we shall suggest in the next chapter, can be called "screen-to-screen" dispute resolution, as opposed to face-to-face dispute resolution. The screen does not currently communicate facial demeanor and gestures. What the screen does allow is, when done well, more effective communication than occurs simply with words or sounds.

Visual communication should not be equated with pictures. Nor should visual communication be equated with graphs and charts or with maps and icons. What we are presented with by creative use of the screen is a range of visual communicative opportunities. This should, and ultimately will be, quite liberating as we learn new ways to combine text and image for purposes of persuasion and explanation. As with many new opportunities, however, we will also be challenged to determine how to use forms of expression that we have probably received little or no training in before.

The third party of the future will require the same level of sensitivity to pictures, images, icons, charts, figures, graphs, scales, tables, diagrams, maps, sketches, blueprints, and colorful animated graphics, as there is to textual or spoken communication. This does not mean that one needs to be able to actually draw any of these items. The ease with which numbers are, even today, transformed into charts illustrates the assistance that the "fourth party" will provide to us. But there will still be a need to learn how to use visual tools in the most effective way, just as we continually face the challenge of expressing ourselves clearly and forcefully when we speak and write.

A More Complex Example

Most of the examples we have used in this book have involved relatively small transactions or fairly simple relationships. The best example of the enabling power of the online environment for graphical communication comes from an extremely complex international negotiation. This was the negotiation between the Bosnian Serb, Croat, and Muslim factions that resulted in the Dayton Peace Accords in 1995.

The negotiations in Dayton were the first to employ digital maps. These maps not only had detailed boundaries that could be adjusted, but could "visualize" terrain. The negotiators were experienced in the use of maps but were also "used to paper maps, the crisp appearance of printed detail, and the flexibility of drawing on their map copy where and when they wished." The digital maps provided computer generated images of terrain and allowed the negotiators to try out different boundary lines. This use of technology contributed significantly to the successful completion of the Dayton negotiation.

What we admire most about the use of maps in Dayton is not how they were used but that the negotiators were willing to learn how to use them. The most challenging aspect of employing ODR in an offline context will be to recognize that the manner in which we have been resolving disputes, even if we have been quite successful, can be enhanced. Mediators and arbitrators need to recognize that however complete their toolkit was a year ago, it is less complete today because the array of available tools is growing. There are skills to be learned, but the greatest obstacle lies in the realm of an unwillingness to spend time exploring the online environment.

The next chapter deals with dispute resolution that occurs exclusively online. Third parties in such disputes have no choice but to try to keep their familiarity with online resources high. Many traditional mediators would like to think that the network is only suitable when there is no face-to-face option. We expect that over time the network will be recognized as one more element that can be employed to bring parties together in any kind of dispute.

6

How Mediators Can Facilitate "Screen-to-Screen" Agreement

A Primer for Conflict Resolution Professionals Entering ODR

Online Arbitration; Online Mediation, *Using the Screen Creatively,*
The Challenges of Using the Screen; **Ethics, Standards, and Competency;**
Skills; *Building and Maintaining Trust, Verbal and Nonverbal Communication,*
Managing Emotions, Active Listening, Asking Questions, Reframing, Reading
and Writing; **Ethics and Standards of Practice,** *Explaining the Process,*
Fees, Transparency, Impartiality, Confidentiality and Privacy, Accessibility;
Conclusion: Building Quality Online Practices.

The ideal mediation process would include online and offline interactions that take advantage of the strengths of each. The last chapter identified several opportunities for using the network to supplement face-to-face encounters. There will be a growing number of online tools that can assist dispute resolution when much of the process is handled quite traditionally. The more flexible any new tool is, the more the potential it will have for wide application.

When the process is exclusively online, we are only beginning to exploit the power of the network. Even existing resources, however, should be quite adequate for many disputes. And just as offline mediation often operates and succeeds with less than perfect levels of convenience, trust, and even expertise, online mediation will also occur at times with less than perfect levels of convenience, trust, or expertise.

In previous chapters, we discussed the nature of the online environment and how that influences the choices that an online mediator might make. In this concluding chapter, we focus on specific issues of ODR practice that need to be understood in order to experiment with and use online resources. Mediating with parties online can be a very different experience than mediating in face-to-face settings. The skills and strategies of experienced offline third parties are not necessarily appropriate or effective in online negotiations. Nor do the traditional standards of practice easily apply in the online environment.

The task of the online mediator, like the task of the offline mediator, must be to employ the most appropriate and powerful verbal and nonverbal tools available. Many of the verbal tools that we have, such as email and Web-based conferencing, are already in common use. For verbal communication, we shall explore below some of the challenges in how to use written language to respond to various kinds of situations that often arise during an online mediation process. Again, the level of interactivity online may not be able to match the level of interactivity in a face-to-face encounter, but the online environment also has some novel resources for enabling the participants to express themselves efficiently and appropriately.

Resources for online nonverbal communication are less familiar than textual tools. While offline nonverbal communication is largely identified with the cues, signals, and other "between the lines" communication, the key to nonverbal online communication and interaction lies in how we employ the screen and what we can learn from the screen. It is intriguing that design of the screen is normally referred to as the inter*face*. This term means that there is influential information on the screen that has nothing to do with the words we see on the screen. This inter*face*, like a person's face, can be employed to communicate meaning and can shape how the verbal content is received.

Just as the meaning of words communicated face to face is influenced by how the words are communicated, words communicated electronically are influenced by how they are displayed. In the last chapter, we identified some of the opportunities for visual communication that are appearing online. The screen, by its appearance and design, is itself an image that functions to structure communication. The screen is the context in which interaction occurs, and it does have an effect on the message. In many ways it is quite analogous to tone of voice and demeanor in that the screen provides a shape and mood to whatever is being communicated. Most importantly, just as voice and demeanor are almost bonded to the actual words being used, the screen is "a part of the conversation rather than an adjunct to it."[1]

One reason we are optimistic about ODR is because there is not simply content, words, and images, but a frame, the screen, around all communication. An important facet of the "fourth party" that we spoke of earlier is the screen, which can add authority, quality, and trust to the online mediation process. Products that use the screen well will enhance the chances for success and add value to the expertise of the mediator. Products that do not recognize the power of the screen will miss out on the numerous ways in which the interface itself can enhance convenience, build trust, and raise expectations that the process will provide value.

We are accustomed to thinking of what appears on the screen as a "window." Yet, unlike a window, the screen is not transparent. Nor can it be easily separated from what appears on it. The screen is also not just background but one of many elements that communicates meaning. We may not have as much control over an interface as we do over some of the content we are actually able to place on the screen, but we can understand some things about the screen that will enable us to use it in ways that can lead to a more effective dispute resolution process.

This chapter is about how you can use screen-to-screen tools for working with the parties to reach resolution. Online, as offline, there is considerable divergence between processes of arbitration and mediation. We shall begin this chapter with a discussion of arbitration, which is an easier process to move online. It is possible to move arbitration online without departing in major ways from the offline model because arbitration is a simpler communication process than mediation. Roles are clearer and exchanges may be fewer. This does not mean that there are not some challenges, but only that overall, it will be easier to develop online arbitration models, and there will be less variation among online arbitration Web sites.

The second part of this chapter is devoted to working with the parties to move toward consensus. Mediation is a process in which the mediator will have many decisions and choices to make as to how to interact online with the parties.

Online Arbitration

The challenges in conducting online arbitration are quite different from the challenges confronting online mediation that we shall discuss below. Arbitration is, in general, a much less complex communications process than mediation, and the technology and software required for arbitration will, as a result, tend to be less complicated. In the simplest arbitrations, software that allows positions to be stated and documents to be shared may provide a sufficient frame for the process. Even in more complicated disputes, the underlying communications process will still, in all likelihood, be less complicated than it is in mediation.

There are situations in which some aspect of a dispute, such as the need to examine an artifact, can pose problems for arbitrations conducted exclusively online. The main challenges to online arbitration, however, lie more in the realm of law than technology. Arbitration leads to authoritative decisions. Some of the authority of these decisions comes from knowing that courts will enforce them. In order for a court to do this, however, there is a need to know which court to turn to and whether all the conditions that the court will look at before it enforces a decision have been satisfied.

The most important set of rules concerning the enforceability of arbitration awards is the New York Convention on the Recognition and Enforcement of Foreign Arbitral Awards of 1958. Most of the questions that might be raised concerning online arbitration concern the arbitration agreement, the arbitration process, and the arbitration award. We are in a time period in which questions are being raised about how different online arbitration is from arbitration in which telephones or fax are relied on, and questions will probably continue to be raised. Even today, however, arbitration conducted through the Internet would seem to meet the general requirements needed to enforce awards. For example:

- *The agreement to arbitrate*—The New York Convention requires an "agreement in writing." Is an agreement formed by the exchange of emails an "agreement in writing"? The Convention specifically states that an exchange of letters or telegrams satisfies the "agreement in writing" requirement. Some early commentators expressed doubt about this, but more recent writings have suggested that email be treated no differently from more tangible forms.[2]

- *The process of arbitration*—The use of the Internet to provide and circulate information and materials should be agreed to explicitly by the parties. Care should also be taken to use reasonable means to protect the confidentiality and authenticity of messages. Digital signatures can be employed if desired, but agreements should also be allowed by clicking on a "submit," "transmit," or "accept" button on a Web site.

  If agreed to by the parties, deliberation of a panel of arbitrators through electronic means should also be permitted. Care should be taken that all members of the panel have sufficient technological skill and resources to participate fully. The fact that deliberations take place exclusively online or through a combination of communications media should also not interfere with the designation of a "seat of arbitration."

Designating a formal place of arbitration can be achieved through agreement of the parties or arbitrators.

- *The arbitration award*—There are jurisdictions that require that the award be in writing. This award may need to be submitted to a court and it is still desirable to have an award that is on paper and that is signed manually by the arbitrators. Doing this, however, does not mean that the parties cannot be notified of the award through electronic means.

Online Mediation

Mediators have expertise in both verbal expression and nonverbal expression. Expression through words is an obviously important component of online mediation and the screen-to-screen model does not enable mediators to employ many of the skills they have been taught for use in face-to-face sessions. Does this mean that online mediation will inevitably be less effective than offline mediation? We don't really think so. As mentioned earlier, we feel that the screen does foster nonverbal communication, albeit not the same kind of nonverbal communication one finds offline. What matters most, for any conflict resolution process, is the right use of the right tools in the right context. Face-to-face intervention has the right tools for many contexts, but not all contexts. The very same statement, as we shall discuss below, can be made about ODR.

When we hear reservations expressed about what we are calling screen to screen, it is often about the limits of text and verbal communication on the screen. After all, face-to-face communication allows one to discern from something other than what is being said whether or not someone is to be trusted or believed. It may reveal how passionately a disputant feels about something. It may even communicate something about whether there is some willingness to compromise. Compared with this rich level of communication, the screen seems to be a negative—something that hides rather than reveals emotion, and that provides no assistance in evaluating sincerity.

What we are calling "screen to screen" cannot and should not be expected to provide the same kind of communication that occurs face to face. It should, however, enable us to take advantage of opportunities that the screen provides to display information, update information, and acquire intelligence based on experience. We generally do not favor the use of real time or "chat" sessions to resolve disputes because these are largely textual exercises that add little that might compensate for the lack of face-to-face contact. When we have experimented with such sessions, the mediators have found that they are rushed, pressured to respond quickly, and less able to control the flow of information among the disputants.[3] They may, in such sessions, be able to exert pressure on the participants to reach settlement, but they have generally felt that such sessions are poor copies of traditional face-to-face meetings.

In such real time sessions, the role of the screen fades away. We may, at some point, find that real-time videoconferencing can indeed duplicate the face-to-face session. What we are most interested in at the moment, however, is in taking advantage of the richness of the display and the powerful technology that connects it to others.

In screen-to-screen mediation, as in many other online activities, a bigger screen is more functional than a small screen. Fortunately, there has been an ongoing increase in the average size of the screens we look at when we are at the computer. There has also been an increase in screen resolution, and as a result, more data can be placed on the screen. We are no longer faced with the screen of text that existed in the PC world for most of its first decade, where all letters were the same size and where one had no control over the appearance of text on the screen.

One of the main attractions of the Apple Macintosh computer was that it allowed images and text to appear together on the screen and for text to be in fonts chosen by the user. The PC did not achieve this capability until the advent of Microsoft Windows. When it did, however, it opened up new opportunities for communicating "beyond words." Our screens now have color, shape, animation, and even sound. We may only be learning to create a rich visual mix out of these ingredients, but to have these elements on machines that are linked to each other via high-speed networks provides a resource we should respect a great deal.

Using the Screen Creatively

We now have an incredible array of choices in how a screen might look and what might be placed on it. Many still assume, unfortunately, that the arrangement of the screen is merely an aesthetic question. We are suggesting that it is also a functional question and that how easy or difficult it might be to resolve a dispute may turn on what appears and also on how it appears.

In the dispute resolution process that SquareTrade has designed, the parties are asked to engage in a period of "direct negotiation" before a mediator is appointed to work with them. SquareTrade has found, quite remarkably, that approximately 80 percent of the disputes filed are resolved through direct negotiation. This is an impressive success rate, particularly since almost all the parties had engaged in some form of negotiation before the complaint was filed. The filing of the complaint is generally a sign that at least one party believes that there is little or no value in any further negotiation.

While a mediator does not participate in the "direct negotiation" process, SquareTrade participates. What does it mean to say that "SquareTrade participates"? The process is called "direct negotiation" but the reality is that it is "mediated negotiation." It is negotiation that takes place mostly through screens designed by SquareTrade, from information supplied by SquareTrade, and in a process structured by SquareTrade. Take a look at Figure 6.1, the first screen someone with a dispute would see. This is not a complaint form but a screen with a bit of information that might be expected to provide encouragement and optimistic expectations for the complainant. The information is a suggestion that 80 percent of the parties are pleased with the process. This, along with the phrase "Building Trust in Transactions," contributes to trust.

FIGURE 6.1. SquareTrade Case Filing Screen.

Copyright 2000, SquareTrade, Inc.

The statement, "the case filing should take 15 minutes," contributes to feelings of convenience. The links on the right side of the screen suggest expertise and experience.

The Challenges of Using the Screen

In the mid-1990s, when we first started thinking about an online mediation process, Web sites were already displaying both text and images easily. We realized fairly quickly that relying on textual communication was inevitable but that, as much as possible, we should endeavor to communicate information visually and invite participants to whenever possible communicate by using methods other than typing text.

The difficulty that many experience in understanding and using on-screen icons in many current applications is a reminder that the development and learning of a new symbolic language can be difficult, that we are still uncomfortable and unfamiliar with many aspects of visual communication, and that text may often remain a preferred and appropriate choice. Yet, just as the face-to-face meeting consists of a continuous flow of verbal and nonverbal elements, the online context must accommodate the nontextual as well, not simply to place colorful or animated objects on screen, and only partly as a form of electronic "body language," but more importantly, as a means of communicating something for which text does not work effectively.

The insertion of visual elements presents several levels of opportunities and challenges.

1. *Attention getting*—This is the most elementary use. It is not uncommon for icons or images to appear on screen to alert the user to some event and to notify the user of some action that should be taken. Red flags, stop signs, and animated light signals do this fairly well.

2. *Envisioning options*—The Web is a branching and hypertextual environment. Mapping mediation sessions also involves identifying branches by depicting connections, dependencies, consequences, and choices.

3. *Temporal issues*—Visualizing changes over time involves some complexity but is not uncommon. The clock is a meaningful object for showing movement, and timelines and graphs to represent events occurring over time are widely employed. In addition, on-screen controls that can be manipulated by users can be employed to clarify and communicate expectations about time frames.

4. *Relationships*—The most challenging areas to develop will be those mechanisms for reflecting relationships. In both the

rulemaking and dispute resolution contexts, the manner in which agreements are formed and consensus is built needs to be represented and shared with participants. The purpose of this is not simply to provide data but to do so in a manner that, as noted earlier, fosters a sense of participating in a shared environment. While temporal issues are often represented graphically, relationships, in the sense of "coming together" or "having a falling out," suggest that there are possibilities for manipulating onscreen space to yield insights and generate solutions and agreements.

Ethics, Standards, and Competency

Screen-to-screen mediation requires not only the acquisition of new skills but also gaining knowledge about new ethical issues and standards of professional practice and competency. The medium requires us to think of the mediator's ethical obligations in different ways. It also requires a rethinking of the accountability that online mediators have to the disputing parties.

For example, during our pilot mediation project with eBay, our mediator received the following message from one of the parties in the middle of the mediation process:

Dear Mediator,

Thank you for all your help. You have been super through all of this and I am very grateful. I know he wants an apology, but the only way he is going to get that is if he sends you the money order for the full amount. When he does so, I will apologize. This man cannot be trusted, but has continued to lie and I have written proof on all of it. He is a liar. This is really bothering me I have been having trouble with controlling my blood pressure and this has not helped. I may seek to sue him if this continues. One other thing, I am offended by his continuous put down of the American way of life and the American Public in general. Perhaps he should have researched his "emigration" more thoroughly. I am sure he hasn't mentioned these remarks to you, but I have kept his anti-American emails to me in my computer and will be happy to send them to you so you can see how prejudiced he is.

I want this matter settled before I end up in the hospital.

Mr. Smith

This email offers a glimpse of the types of challenges online mediators may face. While anger and strong emotion are often expressed in face-to-face mediations, becoming an online dispute resolution practitioner requires the acquisition of some new skills for conflict management as well as an understanding of the standards of practice that are critical to ethical practice. The promise of confidentiality, a core principle in dispute resolution practices, is challenged by the very nature of online technologies where information can be accessed despite the assurances of the online mediator. In the Online Ombuds Office, we have taken the view that the confidentiality that normally applies in face-to-face mediations also applies in the online environment. There is a provision in the User Agreement of the Online Ombuds Office that states:

> The Online Ombuds Office cannot and does not make any promise as to the security or privacy afforded to information while it is in transit over the Internet, and users are herby advised that the Internet is not a secure network. Once information is under the control of the Online Ombuds Office, we will make reasonable efforts to maintain the integrity of the information, including maintaining access to the information and, where agreed, confidentiality of the information, under the terms of the agreement.

As an online mediator, you must respect any request for confidentiality from one of the parties. But, we have interpreted the above to prohibit the mediator from giving, at the request of one of the disputants, copies of all the messages sent to and received from the other—even when confidentiality has not been discussed. Issues of confidentiality will vary depending on the type of online tools you are using, but given the fundamental nature of the online environment, it is clear that ODR promises to give rise to new ethical dilemmas related to confidentiality and other areas of practice. As a result, it is important to develop a set of standards of practice that ensure the quality of these emerging new practices. We begin this discussion with a focus on what skills practitioners need to master in this new field. We then turn to a discussion of a proposed set of standards for ethical ODR practice.

Skills

While there is some variation in the techniques that third party practitioners employ, there are some skills that are fundamental to all dispute resolution practices. These include the ability to build and maintain trust, facility with verbal and nonverbal communication processes, managing emotions, active listening, asking questions, and reframing. In online dispute resolution, third parties will want to utilize the skills of traditional practice as well, but the context of online disputes creates different challenges for their use and mastery.

Building and Maintaining Trust

One of the major responsibilities of a mediator is to build and maintain the trust of the parties. In face-to-face situations, we can do this with tone of voice, body language, phrasing of questions, maintaining our composure in the face of anger emanating from the parties, and maintaining an informal yet structured setting. When two of these tools (tone of voice and body language) are impossible to use, as they are in the online setting, the third party's job becomes much more difficult. One of the things that you will want to decide in determining how to build trust is whether you want to maintain a formal or informal atmosphere. In our project, we have tried both and cannot say that one is absolutely more effective than the other, but we did observe that there was a danger in becoming too informal because it could give the impression that you are siding with the party with whom you are communicating and may interfere with the party's perception of the evolving situation. In face-to-face situations, we can quickly judge and compensate for a party's reaction to jokes, sarcasm, and so on, but online, there are no immediate visual clues, and it becomes much more difficult to recover from something that has broken down some of the trust you have built. You will need to decide in light of the particular case you are mediating, but as a general principle, it might be helpful to maintain a more formal atmosphere, at least with respect to the language we use in communicating with the parties. The following language has been suggested by some SquareTrade mediators, to help establish trust when mediating online:

> To you both, I ask a favor: However this situation arose, it is likely that miscommunication, error, assumptions and a host of other human frailties may be at the root, however much each of you did his honest best—I respectfully request that you try to imagine the most benign of intentions in each other. I have found that Internet dealings easily foster enormous distrust in folk and that as much harm comes from assuming the worst of the other as anything else. I will do my best to help you work this out. I certainly assume that each of you is doing their honest best to come to an agreement you both will find satisfies your concerns.

Another problem with maintaining trust may arise when you are communicating with only one of the parties. The other party has no idea what you are doing— especially if you have to exchange messages three or four times with only one party before getting back to the other. It is easy to forget that, although you are mediating "your heart out" with one of the parties, the other party is getting impatient while waiting to hear from you. The simple solution is to stay in touch with both parties, letting them know what is going on, even if is only to tell one of the parties that you are still discussing the situation with the other. If you get an inquiry from a party, it is advisable to try and respond within twenty-four hours, even if just to say that you will be getting an answer to them soon. It is important to be sure to actually get them an answer. The online environment creates the expectation of instant communication. It is therefore important to respond to messages as quickly as possible and to keep parties informed as to what you are doing. It is important to remember that the online disputant waiting to hear a response is not the same as a disputant waiting in the other room for a private session to end. Building and maintaining trust is a critical part of your job, but it is possible to facilitate an agreement between the parties even when they do not trust each other. Consider other examples from SquareTrade:

> Thank you both for your messages. You have now reached an agreement to give [buyer] a full refund of $752.00 and give the bag back to [seller]. The only thing that needs to be figured out now is how to accomplish this exchange without either of you feeling like you have to give up your bag or money before receiving what you are owed in this exchange. There are a few options:
>
> 1. [buyer] could send the bag c.o.d. and you could both split the charges for this kind of mailing;
> 2. you could agree to a particular date as the day that each of you will mail your respective item to the other; or
> 3. you could agree to meet somewhere and exchange the items in person (this was [seller]'s suggestion, since I understand that you are both in the same area).
>
> Let me know what you both think, and how you feel most comfortable accomplishing this. After you have agreed to a method of exchange, then we can finalize this settlement in an agreement.

These examples illustrate how an online mediator might handle a situation where trust has not been fully achieved but an agreement can nonetheless be reached. The mediator widened the areas of possible settlement without siding with either party, and acted as an advocate of the process itself.

Verbal and Nonverbal Communication

In her book, *The Mind and Heart of the Negotiator*,[4] Leigh Thompson recommends that in online negotiation messages be concise and clear. She points out that people have a great deal of difficulty making sense of messages that are exchanged in face-to-face interactions, and that this is even more of a challenge in online exchanges. Longer messages give people more opportunity to ascribe meaning and innuendo to your query. In addition, long messages try people's patience. Thompson recommends, for example, that an email message fit on a single screen. It is also important to respond to parties in a timely fashion, not simply to build and maintain trust as we pointed out in the previous section, but also to engage parties in the storytelling process that is essential to online communication. People who are using the online medium expect speedy responses and will likely be frustrated and less willing to continue to participate if communication is too slow.

It should be noted that the online mediator does have a resource available that is not present in face-to-face settings; online mediators can keep copies of language they use that seems to have a desired effect. When working asynchronously, there is no reason why mediators should not reuse language that they have used successfully in previous disputes.

Managing Emotions

Strong emotions are invariably expressed in face-to-face interactions. In these environments, the third party can rely on a range of visual and nonverbal cues which can enhance their ability to constructively manage the expression of strong feelings. In online venues, third parties have different challenges, partially because emotions are expressed differently and it is often harder to interpret the emotional meaning and impact of written cues. In her investigation of the behaviors of online negotiators, Thompson found that people involved in negotiations are much more likely to issue threats when communicating via information technology. Given these patterns of communication in online exchanges, the online mediator needs to be not only aware of these tendencies but also needs to set and follow clear behavioral ground rules. As an online mediator, you will need to actively and quickly intervene if and when one or both parties hurl insults. There may be occasions in which it is appropriate to use the telephone to address some of these potential difficulties, but if that is not possible, it might be desirable to have a private electronic exchange with a particularly inflammatory party. It is also important to remember that written electronic communications can be ambiguous and hard to interpret. It is important to clarify, and perhaps reframe and test with the parties, the meaning of a statement before reacting to it or forwarding it to the other party. Most fundamentally, it is essential that you acknowledge the feelings that are being expressed. For example, SquareTrade offers the following sample language:

> Your anger is clear, Ryan, and I do regret that the situation has left you feeling that way. Let's look to the future for a moment.

This type of response should be familiar to offline mediators and a reminder that many of the skills that you have acquired in the past will continue to be useful and appropriate in the online context.

Active Listening

Active listening is a core skill that offline third parties employ in an effort to hear and actively feed back the content and the feeling of a speaker's message. Active listening is critical to trust building and information sharing as it allows the listener to show that they are trying to understand the speaker's story and situation. There are three aspects to active listening: "attending," "paraphrasing," and "identifying feelings." The first of these, "attending," is the most challenging to employ in online mediations because it involves the use of nonverbal indicators such as leaning forward, facial expressions, and physical expressions of affirmation. Obviously, in the online arena one cannot "attend" through the use of body language. The online mediator needs to develop different ways of "attending." An example of this might be a quickly delivered, one-line message of a phrase that shows understanding and concern. Online, one shows their interest and empathy through quick responses using nonjudgmental language. The third subskill, "identifying feelings," is also challenging in online dispute resolution because before you can reflect back and test the emotional stance of a party, you must first figure out what that stance is. Without the speaking context and visual prompts of a face-to-face meeting, the online third party has to rely on an interpretation of a written expression. An online mediator not only has to be skilled in active listening but also in "active reading," which is being able to read the innuendoes of written expression and ask appropriate written questions to effectively identify and attend to feelings. Sometimes, active listening might lead an online mediator to offer comments and reflections about their experience with online conflict. One example of this is in the sample language on active listening that SquareTrade offers its mediators:

> I am sorry to report that [XXXXX] is still extremely irate and is not willing to consider an arrangement where he would send the guitar before receiving payment. I am not sure why his anger level is so high. I have found you to be completely responsive and reasonable to deal with. I can only imagine that it comes from some of the high distrust that I have been seeing in many of buyers and sellers who have dealings online.

There are significant differences when you do not see each other and talk to each other personally. In any event, [XXXXX] does not see this case as one of an honest difference of opinion regarding the condition of the guitar, but rather one of fraud. He is still willing to end the matter and withdraw his complaint, but only if he receives a full refund and money for shipping the guitar back to you. Otherwise, he will continue with his complaint.

Asking Questions

A mediator's effectiveness is often determined by their ability to ask probing, clear, and well-focused questions. Mediators need to ask questions that go beyond what the speaker has stated in order to surface some of the underlying issues and potential areas of mutual concern and interest. These kinds of questions are open-ended, that is, they do not ask for simple yes or no answers. In the online context, mediators have the same goals as their offline counterparts and will need to ask open-ended, probing questions. The challenge for online mediators in employing this technique is that there is a greater likelihood of ambiguity and misinterpretation in written exchanges, and it is more cumbersome to clarify one's meaning. In addition, without the visual cues that often help to elucidate the meaning of a statement, online communications stand by themselves. Online mediators need to take care that their questions are concise and clear. It is also important that you explicitly check with people to make sure they understand the questions asked. Even more challenging is the fact that by searching for underlying issues through open-ended questions, you are inviting people to express their feelings, which may actually exacerbate the situation you are trying to resolve. The face-to-face contact can mitigate or heighten the tension. But in online spaces, when using written words as tools, it is particularly important to try to anticipate what the consequences might be of asking probing questions.

Reframing

This is a process that helps to change the way a party sees an issue. In her manual on mediation skills,[5] Cheryl Picard says that reframing can be used to identify underlying interests, soften demands, modify headlines, decrease threats, and remove emotional or value-laden language. According to Picard, the techniques of reframing include paraphrasing, summarizing, ordering issues in logical sequences, breaking issues into smaller and more manageable sub-issues, removing emotions or value-laden language by stating issues in a nonjudgmental or nonemotional way. Online mediators also need to utilize the technique of reframing. But again, the challenge is to find language that reframes issues in ways that do not create ambiguity and spark "flaming." It might be advisable for example, to reframe issues with the parties separately so that, if there is a misinterpretation that needs to be worked out, it can be done outside of the other party's "online earshot." This relates to the question of what kind of online tool you are using. If you are using email for example, there is no way to stop one party from sending the other a copy of your email exchanges with them; this could have problematic consequences for you as you try to manage this online process.

Reading and Writing

These are skills that are unique to the online third party. While the offline mediator relies on verbal and nonverbal communication and needs to be adept at making meaning from these types of expressions, the online mediator needs to be able to interpret written expressions and gauge reactions and interventions to minimize the potential for conflict escalation and flaming. The online mediator also needs to be able to read and write quickly enough to respond in a timely fashion and, in online exchanges, timely means speedily. People are easily frustrated in online communications, and if they don't get an answer to their message quickly, they are likely to lose trust and make damaging written statements. Sometimes a message from a party may be ambiguous. It is important to check with the party as to its meaning before responding substantively to the message. This search for making meaning of online communications can be further complicated by the fact that you cannot be sure of the identity of the party. You may not know, for example, what their gender, cultural background, or age is, and while this information may not be directly relevant to the dispute, you might make some assumptions about the parties that are inaccurate and could give rise to written comments that one or both of the parties finds offensive. As you formulate your questions and responses and as you interpret the parties' messages, you should try to anticipate their reactions. This is a challenging task because you may have little information about the disputants.

Ethics and Standards of Practice

Recently, we received the following inquiry via email:

Dear Ms. Rifkin,

I am looking for an online mediation service and I saw your Website and was hoping you might be able to assist me. I live in Colorado, my brother lives in Ohio, my sister in Florida and my father, whose health is failing, lives in Massachusetts. It is clear that we are going to have to determine and agree on a number of things before we can figure out how best to take care of my father and preserve his estate. Each of my siblings would like my father to move from Massachusetts to where they are and wants to have control of his assets. I am only concerned that, if my father is to move, he moves to the best place that is available for him and that his assets be used in the most suitable manner for his care. I think we could benefit from mediation but it will not be possible to meet together in one place. I hope you can help us.

Sincerely,

Sidney Winer

As an online mediator, your response to such an inquiry should be carefully crafted to insure that it meets a standard of ethical practice and competency. This can be accomplished in a number of ways as long as the parties are given clear and accessible information about the process, your fees, transparency, impartiality, confidentiality and privacy, record-keeping, and accessibility. One way to partially ensure that you are conforming to appropriate standards of practice is to adopt, incorporate, and make visible to the parties an existing set of professional standards like the Society for Professionals in Dispute Resolution's (SPIDR) Ethical Standards of Professional Responsibility. But these standards are not completely adequate to cover the needs of an online mediator and online disputants. You should pay particular attention to the following areas and make sure that you offer clear information to the parties about these matters.

Explaining the Process

It is extremely important that you explain to all of the parties how the process is going to be structured. You will need to make clear, for example, how the second party will be contacted and asked to respond, how the first party will be informed about this response, and the timeframe within which this initial part of the process will take place. It is also important that you give the parties clear information about the timeframe of the overall process. Although this information should be part of your written exchanges with them, it is advisable that you develop and make easily available a documented description of the process you are proposing to use with them. For example, in the example above, you should be able to direct all of the potential parties in this matter to a place where they could read a description of your service and the online service you offer, and you should then confirm that they have each read and understood it before you proceed with the mediation.

Fees

Online dispute resolvers should provide the parties with full disclosure of all fees, the basis of such fees, how the fee arrangement is structured, and what the costs to each party will be. If you are using a flat fee arrangement, you should make that clear and disclose in advance other possible fee arrangements, such as referral fees, contingency fees, commissions, and so on. In the example at the beginning of this chapter, the inquiry did not specifically ask about fees. The online mediator, however, has a duty to affirmatively disclose the fee structure to all parties, even if this matter is not raised by any of the parties.

Transparency

The online practitioner may well have to meet a higher standard of practice on this issue than their offline counterparts. Because the online environment can mask a lot of information about the identity of the parties and the mediator, it is particularly important that the online mediator give enough information about himself that potential users of the service are sufficiently informed about the credentials of the provider as well as the nature of the service being proffered. Nora Femenia and a group of other mediators have proposed that online dispute resolvers provide annually updated statistics that include how many disputes they have handled, what percentage of those disputes have resulted in agreements, typical and maximum times it takes to reach an agreement, and the minimum and average fees for each party.

Impartiality

We recommend that online dispute resolvers follow the SPIDR standards on this point, which state:

> The neutral must maintain impartiality toward all parties. Impartiality means freedom from favoritism or bias either by

word or action, and a commitment to serve all parties as opposed to a single party. The dispute resolution process belongs to the parties. The neutral has no vested interest in terms of a settlement, but must be satisfied that agreements in which he or she has participated will not impugn the integrity of the process.

The challenge for ODR practitioners is that it may be harder to practice neutrality through online communications because it may be harder to ascertain how the parties are interpreting your messages. Bias may be expressed differently, and perhaps inadvertently, in written communications, and it may be more difficult to clarify and correct misperceptions that can arise in online exchanges. That is why it is important for the online mediator to respond in a timely and frequent fashion to messages and to explicitly check with the parties during the process about their interpretation of and reaction to the communications they send and receive.

In the example above, it is important that we get equal information from all the potential parties and not just from the person who contacted us first. To ensure impartiality in online mediation, you will also need to ensure that all parties can participate equally and competently in an online process. If one or more cannot, either because of lack of access to computers or lack of technological skill, then it is advisable to either use a different process or to have the parties participate through different means. You could have some parties meet face to face, via telephone, or conceivably through videoconferencing. Using different technologies may complicate your ability to be impartial because you will have different responses to people you speak with in person or on the phone or to those with whom you communicate online. It is important that you monitor your own reactions in these situations and continually gauge the parties' reactions to your interventions and the overall process.

In the case we illustrated, it would be important to think about how the father's interests could be represented in this process. He might be too infirm to fully participate in any kind of dialogue, but he may also not be competent with computers. In either case, the mediator will have to raise that issue with all of the parties and figure out how to meet this need. This is an example of when a mediator may have to represent the interests of a particular party. This challenges the general precept that mediators assure impartiality by not showing bias toward any one party. Yet, in an instance such as this, the mediator may be perceived as showing bias toward the father by representing his interests to the others. Before the substantive discussion in such a case can proceed, this matter will have to be raised and agreed upon by all the participants.

Confidentiality and Privacy

It is critical that an online dispute resolver explicitly state how information provided by the parties will be used. It is also critical that you get their explicit acknowledgment that they understand this information and consent to participate under the conditions you explicate. It is advisable that their consent be expressed online either by filling out a form or clicking on a radio button or some other electronic mechanism, which gives them access to read and assent to the policy and gives you the ability to confirm their agreement and assent.

Accessibility

Any dispute resolution process needs to ensure that all potential parties have equal access to the process being proposed. For example, mediators need to make sure that all participants can speak in the language being used, and that might mean the need for a translator. In online settings, in addition to concerns about language you must be sure that the parties are able to participate using the technology being employed. To do this, you will have to determine the capacity of the parties and to get their explicit consent to the mode of communication being employed. If one or more of the parties are not comfortable with the proposed software, then either another mode of communication needs to be used or the parties need to be trained to competently use the proposed technology before the mediation can begin.

Conclusion: Building Quality Online Practices

The online dispute resolver must follow a professional code and clearly state which code is being followed before the parties agree to proceed with the process. It is also important, just as in offline practices, that the online mediator state explicitly where their responsibilities end. The online mediator needs to state what compliance mechanisms are available before, during, and after the process and if they will be reporting noncompliance to any agency or other authority. While these obligations are consistent with offline practices, the online practitioner is under an even greater obligation to disclose information because of the environment in which they are working. An online mediator needs to take care to give explicit information about their policies and practices because their accountability is harder to ensure. It is easy to bill oneself as an online mediator, and the risks for online consumers and parties is greater than for offline consumers. It is also easy to make mistakes using technology. For example, an online mediator could accidentally send a copy of an email message to a third party who is unconnected to the case. This occurred in a situation that one of our Center's mediators was handling. If such a mistake does take place, it is not necessarily fatal to the integrity of the mediation process, but it is important that you get back to the party immediately and acknowledge the error. For example, in our case, the mediator recognized her mistake within five minutes of sending the party the email message.

This is the message that the mediator sent as soon as the discovery was made:

Dear Cynthia,

My previous email to you contained an error. I inadvertently added Joseph Green, one of my mediation supervisors, to the copy list. Sorry for the mistake. Being human, I do make errors from time to time and hope you will be understanding of that. I will do my best to use extra care in the future.

Sarah

The party emailed the mediator back shortly thereafter with the following reply.

Dear Sarah,

Thanks for giving me notice of your mistake. I appreciate your honesty and admission of human error. It's not a problem. I look forward to getting the mediation process under way.

Hope to hear from you soon.

Cynthia

Obviously, this was a mistake that was easy to fix. However, not every situation will be that simple. The point to keep in mind is to understand the environment in which you are working so you will be able to exercise competency and integrity not only as a mediator but also with the technology. Be alert and respond quickly and appropriately if and when you make an error of judgment or of substance. Ethical violations can occur unwittingly, and it is your job to know when such a violation has either occurred or is likely to.

In this chapter, we have delineated some of the critical skills and competencies that you will need to learn to be an effective and responsible online dispute resolver. This is an exciting and important arena. As more and more people do business online and use the Internet for social interaction, disputes are inevitable. Increasingly, there will be a need for competent online problem solvers. We encourage you to embrace this new space for dispute resolution and to learn more about opportunities for and the challenges of online dispute resolution practices.

Appendix 1: Online Literature and Resources About ODR

The following list includes articles, papers, reports, and some organizational resources that can be found on the World Wide Web. Updated versions of this list will be available at http://www.umass.edu/dispute/bib.htm.

Articles and Papers

The Berkman Center for Internet & Society, Harvard Law School, "Pressing Issues II: Understanding and Critiquing ICANN's Policy Agenda." [http://cyber.law.harvard.edu/icann/pressingissues2000/briefingbook/index.asp]. November 2000.

Bordone, R. C., "Electronic Online Dispute Resolution: A Systems Approach—Potential." *Harv. Negotiation L. Rev.*, 1998, 175–211. [http://eon.law.harvard.edu/h2o/property/jurisdiction/bordoneedit.html]

Cabell, D., *ICANN UDRP Resources*. [http://eon.law.harvard.edu/udrp/library.html].

Center for Information Technology and Dispute Resolution, University of Massachusetts. *Five eBay Mediation Transcripts*. [http://www.disputes.net/cyberweek2000/ebay/ebayintro.htm]. April 1999.

Center for Information Technology and Dispute Resolution, University of Massachusetts. *Cyberweek 2000 Mediation Simulation Transcript*. [http://www.disputes.net/cyberweek2000/tuefeb15.htm]. February 2000.

Cole, S. J. and Underhill, C. I. *Protecting Consumers in Cross-Border Transactions: A Comprehensive Model for Alternative Dispute Resolution.* Arlington, VA: Council of Better Business Bureaus.
[http://ilpf.org/confer/present00/blumenfeld_pr/blumenfeld1_pr.htm].
September 2000.

DeStephen, D., and Helie, J. "Online Dispute Resolution: Implications for the ADR Profession." [http://www.mediate.com/articles/helie1.cfm].

Fouchard, P. "Alternative Dispute Résolution et Arbitrage: L'évolution des modes de règlement des litiges du commerce international."
[http://www.oecd.org/dsti/sti/it/secur/act/Online_trust/fouchard.pdf].

Gibson, C. "Arbitration In Intellectual Property Disputes." *California International Practitioner.* 8 (1).
[http://web72330.ntx.net/articles/arbitration_ip_intl.html]. Spring-Summer 1997.

Gellman, R. "A Brief History of the Virtual Magistrate Project: The Early Months." [http://mantle.sbs.umass.edu/vmag/GELLMAN.HTM]. May 1996.

Gilbert, P. "On Space, Sex And Stalkers." *Sexuality and Cyberspace,* 17.
[http://www.echonyc.com/~women/Issue17/art-gilbert.html].

Goldsmith, J., and Lessig, L. "Grounding the Virtual Magistrate."
[http://mantle.sbs.umass.edu/vmag/groundvm.htm]. May 1996.

Granat, R. S. "Creating An Environment for Mediating Disputes On the Internet." Paper prepared for NCAIR Conference on Online Dispute Resolution, Washington, DC. [http://mantle.sbs.umass.edu/vmag/ granat.htm]. May 1996.

Grossman, W. *Net. Wars.* New York: NYU Press.
[http://www.nyupress.nyu.edu/netwars.html] 1997.

Hague Conference on Private International Law, *Report from September 1999 Geneva Roundtable on Electronic Commerce and Private International Law.*
[http://www.hcch.net/e/workprog/e-comm.html]. April 2000.

Hill, R. "On-line Arbitration: Issues and Solutions." *Arbitration International.*
[http://www.umass.edu/dispute/hill.htm]. December 1998.

ICANN Uniform Dispute Resolution Policy.
[http://www.icann.org/udrp/udrp.html].

Johnson, D. R. "Dispute Resolution in Cyberspace."
[http://www.eff.org/pub/Legal/Arbitration/
online_dispute_resolution_johnson.article]. 1994.

Johnson, D. R. and Post, D. G. "Law And Borders–The Rise of Law in Cyber-space." *Stanford Law Review*, 48, 1367.
[http://www.cli.org/X0025_LBFIN.html]. 1996.

Katsh, E. "Dispute Resolution In Cyberspace." *Conn. L. Rev*, 1996, 28(4), 953–980. [http://www.umass.edu/legal/articles/uconn.html].

Katsh, E. Introduction to *The Electronic Media and the Transformation of Law*.
New York: Oxford U. Press.
[http://www.umass.edu/legal/katsh/em_intr1.html]. 1989.

Katsh, E. Introduction to *Law in a Digital World*. New York: Oxford U. Press.
[http://www.umass.edu/legal/katsh/dw_intr1.html]. 1989.

Katsh, E. "Online Dispute Resolution." In J. Aresty and J. Silkenat (ed.), *Guide to International Business Negotiations*. Chicago: American Bar Association.
[http://www.umass.edu/cyber/aresty.html]. 2000.

Katsh, E. "The Online Ombuds Office: Adapting Dispute Resolution to Cyberspace." [http://mantle.sbs.umass.edu/vmag/katsh.html]. May 1996.

Katsh, E., Rifkin, J., and Gaitenby, A. "E-Commerce, E-Disputes, and E-Dispute Resolution: In the Shadow of 'eBay Law,'" *Ohio State J. of Dispute Resolution*, 2000, 15(3), 705–734. [http://www.umass.edu/cyber/katsh.pdf].

Mnookin, J. L. "Virtual(ly) Law: The Emergence of Law in LambdaMOO," *Journal of Computer-Mediated Communication*: 2(1), 1996.
[http://www.ascusc.org/jcmc/vol2/issue1/lambda.html].

Mudd, C. "Cybercourt: A Virtual Resolution of Differences or An Alternative Proposal for Law and Order in Cyberspace."
[http://www.mudd.org/professional/articlesclm/cybercourt.html]. 1995.

Olmstead, W. "Electronic Dispute Resolution at the NRC."
[http://mantle.sbs.umass.edu/vmag/OLMST.HTM]. May 1996.

Perritt, H. "Electronic Dispute Resolution: An NCAIR Conference." [http://mantle.sbs.umass.edu/vmag/PERRITT.HTM]. May 1996.

Pilcher, R. "Trust and Reliance—Enforcement and Compliance: Enhancing Consumer Confidence in the Electronic Marketplace." [http://www.oecd.org/dsti/sti/it/secur/act/online_trust/Consumer_Confidence.p df]. May 2000.

Post, D. "Engineering a Virtual Magistrate System." [http://mantle.sbs.umass.edu/vmag/DGP2.HTM]. May 1996.

Rule, C. "New Mediator Capabilities in Online Dispute Resolution." [http://www.mediate.com/articles/rule.cfm].

SchWeber, C. "The Use of Technology in Conflict Resolution." [http://www.batnet.com/oikoumene/arbtadr.html]. October 1994.

Thiessen, E. "Beyond Win-Win in Cyberspace." OneAccord Publication: *Ohio State J. of Dispute Resolution*, 2000, 15(3), 643. [http://www.smartsettle.com/more/beyond/BeyondWinWin.html].

United Nations Convention on the Recognition and Enforcement of Foreign Arbitral Awards of 1958 ("New York Convention"). [http://www.internationaladr.com/tc121.htm].

Valley, K. "The Electronic Negotiator." *Harvard Business Review*, January–February 2000, 16-17. [http://www.mediate.com/articles/valley.cfm].

van den Heuvel, E. "Online Dispute Resolution as a Solution to Cross-Border E-Disputes: An Introduction to ODR." [http://www.oecd.org/ dsti/sti/it/secur/act/online_trust/VanHeuvel.pdf]. August 2000.

Governmental and Organizational Papers and Reports

American Arbitration Association, *eCommerce Dispute Management Protocol.* [http://www.adr.org/rules/guides/ecomm_protocol.html]. January 2001.

Asia Pacific Economic Cooperation (APEC), E-Commerce Steering Group. *Report and proposals for action following the APEC workshop on consumer protection held in Bangkok on 20 July 2000.* [http://www.ecommerce.gov/apec/meeting/072000/bangkokfollowup.html]. July 2000.

BBBOnLine. *Code of Online Business Practices.* [http://www.bbbonline.org/code/code.asp]. October 2000.

Consumers International. *Disputes in Cyberspace Report, (Executive Summary).* [http://www.consumersinternational.org/campaigns/electronic/sumadr-final.html]. December 2000.

CPR Business-To-Business E-Commerce Initiative. [http://www.cpradr.org/ecommerce.html]. 2000.

Electronic Commerce and Consumer Protection Group. *Guidelines for Merchant-to-Consumer Transactions.* [http://www.ecommercegroup.org/guidelines.html]. June 2000.

European Commission Recommendation 98/257/EC. *Principles Applicable To The Bodies Responsible For Out-Of-Court Settlement Of Consumer Disputes.* [http://europa.eu.int/comm/consumers/policy/developments/acce_just/acce_just02_en.html].

European Commission Report: *Out-of-Court Dispute Settlement Systems for E-Commerce: The Report from the Workshop held in Brussels on 21 March 2000.* [http://dsa-isis.jrc.it/ADR/WS-2103-report.pdf]. March 2000.

Federal Trade Commission. *Summary of June 2000 Public Workshop hosted by the U.S. Department of Commerce and the U.S. Federal Trade Commission, "Alternative Dispute Resolution for Consumer Transactions in a Borderless Online Marketplace."* [http://www.ftc.gov/bcp/altdisresolution/index.htm]. November 2000.

Global Business Dialogue for Electronic Commerce (GBDe). *Alternative Dispute Resolution Paper.* [http://www.gbde.org/library/adr.doc]. September 2000.

International Chamber of Commerce. *Out-Of-Court Settlement Of Disputes Concerning E-Commerce Consumer Transactions: An Inventory Of Current Approaches.* [http://www.oecd.org/dsti/sti/it/secur/act/online_trust/ ICCInventory.doc]. September 2000.

Trans Atlantic Consumer Dialogue. *Alternative Dispute Resolution in the Context of Electronic Commerce Recommendation.*
[http://www.tacd.org/ecommercef.html#adr]. February 2000.

More General Online Resources

ADRonline Monthly. [http://www.umass.edu/dispute/adronline.html].

ADR Cyberweek. [http://www.umass.edu.cyber]

ADRworld. [http://www.adrworld.com].

American Bar Association, Section of Dispute Resolution.
[http://www.abanet.org/dispute/dispute.html].

Conflict Resolution Information Source. [http://www.crinfo.org/].

Dispute-res listserv. [http://aaron.sbs.umass.edu/center/listserv.html].

Mediate.com. [http://www.mediate.com].

Appendix 2: ODR Programs and Ventures

Note: Online Dispute Resolution is, like most Internet-based commercial arenas, one that changes rapidly. The following list is intended to provide a quick view of the field as of February 2001. A more current version can be found at http://www.umass.edu/dispute/odrlist.htm. In the list below, (BB) means that the method of resolution occurs largely through the blind bidding process described in Chapter Two.

1-2-3 Settle (http://www.123Settle.com) (BB)

AllSettle (http://www.allsettle.com) (BB)

Better Business Bureau Online (http://www.bbbonline.org)

ClicknSettle (http://www.clicknsettle.com) (BB)

CyberArbitration (http://www.cyberarbitration.com)

Cybercourt (http://www.cybercourt.com)

Cybersettle (http://www.cybersettle.com)

eResolution (http://www.eresolution.ca)

iCourthouse (http://www.icourthouse.com)

Electronic Consumer Dispute Resolution (ECODIR)
    (http://www.fundp.ac.be/recherche/projets/fr/00299002.html)

iLevel (http://www.ilevel.com)

Internet Neutral (http://www. internetneutral.com)

Internet Ombudsman (http://www.internetombudsmannen.se)

Iris Mediation (http://www.iris.sgdg.org/mediation)

Mediation Arbitration Resolution Services (MARS)
(http://www.resolvemydispute.com)

New Court City (http://www.newcourtcity.com) (BB)

Nova Forum (http://www.nova forum.com)

Online Mediators (http://www.onlinemediators.com)

Online Ombuds Office (http://www.ombuds.org)

OnlineDisputes, Inc. (http://www.onlinedisputes.org)

Resolution Forum Inc. (http://www.resolutionforum.org)

ResolveItNow (http://www.resolveitnow.com) (BB)

SettleOnline (http://www.settleonline.com) (BB)

SettleSmart (http://www.settlesmart.com) (BB)

SquareTrade (http://www.squaretrade.com)

The Virtual Magistrate (http://www.vmag.org)

USSettle (http://www.ussettle.com) (BB)

WEBdispute.com (http://www.webdispute.com)

Webmediate.com (http://www.webmediate.com)

European Advertising Standards Alliance
(http://www.easa-alliance.org)

Appendix 3: CPR Institute for Dispute Resolution

Sample Domain Name Dispute Decision

Administrative Panel Decision Under the ICANN Uniform Domain Name Dispute Resolution Policy

Note: This is a representative arbitration decision under the ICANN Uniform Dispute Resolution Policy (UDRP) discussed in Chapter Two. These disputes always involve a trademark holder (the complainant) versus a person who registered a domain name (the respondent). For an arbitrator to take away the domain name and award it to the trademark holder, the arbitrator must find a violation of the ICANN policy. The relevant section of the policy is paragraph 4(a), which is included below in the arbitrator's opinion. This case involved five domain names and the arbitrator found that the respondent violated the policy in regard to two of the names. All arbitrator decisions under the UDRP are required to be posted on the Web and can be found at http://www.icann.org/udrp/udrp.htm.

COMPLAINANTS

REED PUBLISHING
(NEDERLAND)
B.V. AND REED ELSEVIER
INC.
275 Washington Street
Newton, Massachusetts
United States of America
Telephone: 617-558-4227
Fax: 617-558-4649
E-mail:
henryhorbaczewski@reed-
elsevier.com

RESPONDENT

SELECT GOURMET
FOODS INC.
15022 Juanita Drive, NE
Kenmore, Washington
United States of America
Telephone: 206-528-0332
Fax: 425-487-2749
E-mail: sgfoods@yahoo.com

Before M. Scott Donahey, **Arbitrator**
File Number: CPR004
Date of Commencement: July 27, 2000

Domain Names:
   whoiswhoinamerica.com
   whoiswhointheworld.com
   whoiswhoinmedicine.com
   whoiswhoinlaw.com
   whoiswhoinpolitics.com
Registrar: Network Solutions, Inc.
Arbitrator: M. Scott Donahey

Procedural History

The Complaint was filed with CPR on July 21, 2000, and, after review for administrative compliance, served on the respondent on July 27, 2000. The Respondent did not file a Response on or before August 16, 2000. However, on August 22, 2000, CPR received by Fax a letter with attachments from the Respondent which was in the nature of an informal Response. M. Scott Donahey was appointed Arbitrator pursuant to the Uniform Domain Name Dispute Resolution Policy (UDRP) and Rules promulgated by the Internet Corporation for Domain Names and Numbers (ICANN). The Panel did not consider the informal Response, both because it was late and because it failed to include the certification required by Uniform Rules, Rule 5. Edgar Rice Burroughs, Inc. v. Adtel Communications, ICANN Case No. D2000-0115; EAuto, Inc. v. Available-Domain-Names.com, d/b/a Intellectual-Assets.com, Inc., ICANN Case No. D2000-0120. Upon the written submitted record including the Complaint and Annexes thereto, the Panel finds as follows:

Findings

Respondent's registered domain name,<whoiswhoinamerica.com>, was registered with Network Solutions, Inc. on December 25, 1999. Respondent's registered domain names, <whoiswhointheworld.com>, <whoiswhoinlaw.com>, <whoiswhoinpolitics.com>, and <whoiswhoinmedicine.com>, were registered with Network Solutions, Inc. on December 26, 1999. In registering the names, Respondent agreed to submit to this forum to resolve any dispute concerning the domain names, pursuant to the UDRP.

The UDRP provides, at Paragraph 4(a), that each of three findings must be made in order for a Complaint to prevail:

i. Respondent's domain name must be identical or confusingly similar to a trademark or service mark in which complainant has rights; and

ii. Respondent has no rights or legitimate interests in respect of the domain name; and

iii. Respondent's domain name has been registered and is being used in bad faith.

Identity/Confusing Similarity: Complainant alleges that the domain names at issue are identical or confusingly similar to

Complainant's trademarks, WHO'S WHO IN AMERICA, WHO'S WHO IN THE WORLD, WHO'S WHO IN MEDICINE AND HEALTHCARE, WHO'S WHO IN AMERICAN POLITICS, and WHO'S WHO IN AMERICAN LAW which apply to publications in the nature of a directory.

The Panel finds that the domain names <whoiswhoinamerica.com> and <whoiswhointheworld.com> are virtually identical and confusingly similar to Complainant's marks WHO'S WHO IN AMERICA and WHO'S WHO IN THE WORLD. Nandos International Limited v. M. Fareed Farukhi, ICANN Case No. D2000–0225; DFO, Inc. v. Christian Williams, ICANN Case No. D2000–0181. The panel also finds that the domain name <whoiswhoinmedicine.com> is confusingly similar to Complainant's mark WHO'S WHO IN MEDICINE AND HEALTHCARE. Neither the mark, nor the domain name are limited geographically, and one who is seeking information regarding Complainant's publication is likely to be confused when he or she arrives at the parked homepage to which <whoiswhoinmedicine.com> resolves and would likely assume that a web page produced by Complainant has not yet been constructed. Complaint, Annex L. Yahoo! Inc. v. David Ashby, D2000–0241.

However, the Panel finds that the domain names <whoiswhoinlaw.com> and <whoiswhoinpolitics.com> are not confusingly similar to Complainant's marks WHO'S WHO IN AMERICAN LAW and WHO'S WHO IN AMERICAN POLITICS. Unlike the marks, which are expressly limited geographically, the two domain names at issue are not so limited. Indeed, Complainant includes in its submissions examples of numerous publications from other companies that utilize the "who's who" format with and without geographical limitations (e.g., Who's Who In Society, Who's Who In New York, Who's Who, Who's Who in Electroneurodiagnostics, Who's Who In International Organizations, etc.) Sport Soft Golf, Inc. v. Sites to Behold Ltd., ICANN Case No. FA00060000094976.

The Panel therefore concludes that the registered domain names <whoiswhoinamerica.com>, <whoiswhointheworld.com>, and <whoiswhoinmedicine.com> are identical or confusingly similar to Complainant's protected marks, and that the registered domain names <whoiswhoinlaw.com> and <whoiswhoinpolitics. com> are not identical or confusingly similar to Complainant's protected marks.

Rights and Legitimate Interests: Complainant alleges and Respondent has failed to deny that Respondent has no rights or legitimate interest with respect to the domain names at issue. Alcoholics Anonymous World Services, Inc. v. Raymond, ICANN Case No. D2000–0007; Ronson Plc v. Unimetal Sanayai veTic. A.S., ICANN Case No. D2000–0011.

The Panel therefore concludes that Respondent does not have rights or legitimate interests in respect of the domain names still at issue, namely <whoiswhoinamerica.com>, <whoiswhointhe-world.com>, and <whoiswhoinmedicine.com>.

Bad Faith: In support of the contention of Respondent's bad faith registration and use, Complainant notes that Respondent has registered multiple names, in addition to those at issue, which are unrelated either to Respondent's business or to each other, suggesting an improper motive, and that Respondent failed to change its conduct after receiving notification of infringement from Complainant.

Paragraph 4(b) of the UDRP provides that indications of bad faith include, without limitation, (a) registration for the purposes of selling, renting or transferring the domain name to the Complainant for value in excess of Respondent's cost; (b) a pattern of registration in order to prevent Complainant from reflecting the mark in a corresponding domain name; (c) registration for the primary purpose of disrupting the business of a competitor; or (d) an intentional attempt to attract, for commercial gain, Internet users to Respondent's web site by creating a likelihood of confusion with Complainant's mark as to the source, sponsorship, affiliation or endorsement of Respondent's web site or location, or of a product or service on Respondent's web site or location.

The domain names registered by Respondent are typically generic or descriptive in nature (e.g., <howtomakealot-ofmoney.com>, <topfivechefs.com>, <truffleoil.com>, <whoiswho-inthefoodworld.com>, <feedingthehungry.com>, <howtofinda-gooddoctor.com>, etc.). The Panel finds that the mere registration of multiple generic or descriptive domain names, without more, does not constitute bad faith registration and use under ¶4(b)(ii), nor does such registration suggest an improper motive. LIBRO AG v. NA Global Link Limited, ICANN Case No. D2000–0186; Microcell Solutions Inc. v. B-Seen Design Group Inc., ICANN Case No. AF-0131.

Moreover, Complainant indicates, without expressly stating, that Respondent contacted Complainant following the letters which Complainant sent, and that some attempts to resolve their differences followed. Complaint, ¶18, last sentence, at 5–6. As Respondent did not attempt to conceal its identity or to hide from Complainant, the Panel does not find that Complainant has met its burden in establishing bad faith registration and use merely from the fact that the parties could not resolve their dispute.

However, two of Complainant's marks are so well known that it is impossible to believe that anyone living in America for any length of time could have been unaware of them. WHO'S WHO IN AMERICA has been in use since 1899, and WHO'S WHO IN THE WORLD has been in use since 1970. Registration of such well known marks as domain names could not have been done in good faith, and any use to which they would be put would constitute bad faith use under the policy. The Panel therefore concludes that Respondent did not register and use the domain name <whoiswhoinmedicine.com> in bad faith, as that term is defined in the ICANN Policy, but did register and use the domain names

<whoiswhoinamerica.com> and <whoiswhointheworld.com> in bad faith.

Conclusion

In light of the findings above that (a) the registered domain names <whoiswhoinlaw.com> and <whoiswhoinpolitics.com> are not identical or confusingly similar to Complainant's protected marks, but that the registered domain names <whoiswhoinamerica.com>, <whoiswhointheworld.com>, and <whoiswhoinmedicine.com> are identical or confusingly similar to Complainant's protected marks; (b) Respondent does not have rights or legitimate interest with respect to the three remaining domain names at issue; and (c) Respondent did not register and use the domain name <whoiswhoinmedicine.com> in bad faith, as that term is defined in the ICANN Policy, but that Respondent did register and use the domain names <whoiswhoinamerica.com> and <whoiswhointheworld.com> in bad faith, the Panel finds in favor of the Respondent as to the domain names <whoiswhoinlaw.com>, <whoiswhoinpolitics.com>, and <whoiswhoinmedicine.com>, and the Panel finds in favor of the Complainant as to the domain names <whoiswhoinamerica.com> and <whoiswhointheworld.com>.

Remedy

Complainant's request to transfer the domain names <whoiswhoinlaw.com>, <whoiswhoinmedicine.com>, and <whoiswhoinpolitics.com> is hereby DENIED.

Complainant's request to transfer the domain names <whoiswhoinamerica.com> and <whoiswhointheworld.com> is hereby GRANTED, and those two domain names shall be transferred to Complainant Reed Publishing (Nederland) B.V.

	August 29, 2000
Signature of Arbitrator	Date

Appendix 4: SquareTrade Direct Negotiation Process

Slide 1: Filing a Complaint

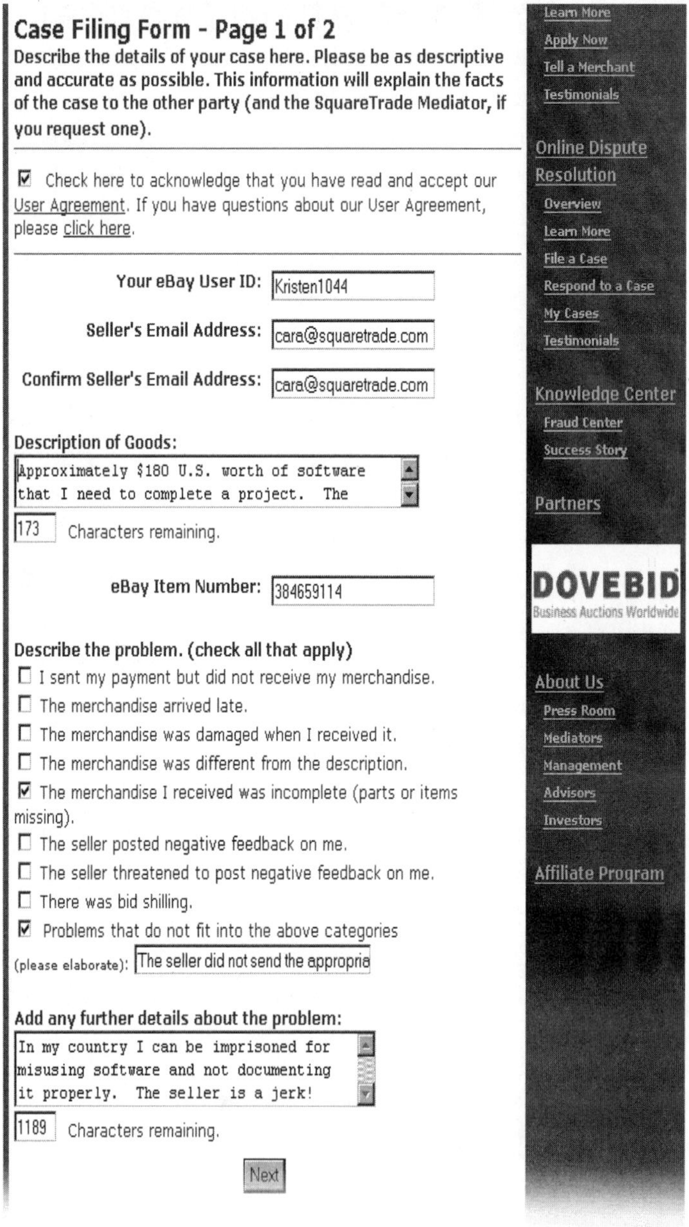

Case Filing Form - Page 1 of 2

Describe the details of your case here. Please be as descriptive and accurate as possible. This information will explain the facts of the case to the other party (and the SquareTrade Mediator, if you request one).

☑ Check here to acknowledge that you have read and accept our User Agreement. If you have questions about our User Agreement, please click here.

Your eBay User ID: `Kristen1044`

Seller's Email Address: `cara@squaretrade.com`

Confirm Seller's Email Address: `cara@squaretrade.com`

Description of Goods:

`Approximately $180 U.S. worth of software that I need to complete a project. The`

`173` Characters remaining.

eBay Item Number: `384659114`

Describe the problem. (check all that apply)
☐ I sent my payment but did not receive my merchandise.
☐ The merchandise arrived late.
☐ The merchandise was damaged when I received it.
☐ The merchandise was different from the description.
☑ The merchandise I received was incomplete (parts or items missing).
☐ The seller posted negative feedback on me.
☐ The seller threatened to post negative feedback on me.
☐ There was bid shilling.
☑ Problems that do not fit into the above categories
(please elaborate): `The seller did not send the appropria`

Add any further details about the problem:

`In my country I can be imprisoned for misusing software and not documenting it properly. The seller is a jerk!`

`1189` Characters remaining.

[Next]

(Sidebar navigation)

Learn More
Apply Now
Tell a Merchant
Testimonials

Online Dispute Resolution
Overview
Learn More
File a Case
Respond to a Case
My Cases
Testimonials

Knowledge Center
Fraud Center
Success Story

Partners

DOVEBID
Business Auctions Worldwide

About Us
Press Room
Mediators
Management
Advisors
Investors

Affiliate Program

Slide 2: Automatic Notification

Respondents are automatically notified

Hello,

SquareTrade was recently contacted by Kristen Anderson
regarding:

 eBay Item Number: 384659119
 Merchandise Description: Approximately $180 U.S. worth of software that I
need to complete a project. The seller has cheated me. I don't understand
why she would do this. I am outraged. She didn't send me the appropriate
registration documentation.
 Problem: The merchandise I received was incomplete (parts or items
missing).

The SquareTrade service is a free and simple way for individuals and
businesses
to resolve issues with online transactions. This service also offers the
opportunity to remove negative feedback to help sellers and buyers protect
their reputations and maintain positive business relationships.

We currently only have the information provided by Kristen and it
is important that you share your point of view. To respond, please do the
following:

1. Click on the link
    http://cf.squaretrade.com/response_form/Default.cfm?cid=1777770585
       and enter your email address.
2.   Fill in New User Registration to create a password. The password will
    ensure that all correspondence between you and Kristen will
    remain secure.
3.   Review the information provided by Kristen and choose the link
    "Respond to this Case".

You can learn more about SquareTrade at www.squaretrade.com.

Sincerely,

SquareTrade Customer Support

Build Trust, Build Loyalty with the SquareTrade Seal.
Learn more at http://www.squaretrade.com

Copyright 2000, SquareTrade, Inc.

Slide 3: Entering Direct Negotiation

Building Trust in Transaction

Home | Log Off | Help

SQUARE TRADE

Online Dispute Resolution Process

Direct Negotiation
Welcome Cara Cherry Lisco ...

You may communicate with Kristen Anderson by entering a message below.

Please enter your message in 4,500 characters or less.

0   Characters remaining.

post message

Please keep in mind that all communications in this process are confidential. Please refer to the User Confidentiality Agreement for details.

Sender	Date	Message
cara@ squaretrade.com	Mon, Nov 20, 2000 12:54 PM	Ms. Anderson, The item description did not say this was new software. There was no way for me to know that you needed new software with documentation, otherwise I wouldn't have sold it to you. I can't send you the documentation. Ms. Lisco

back to the Case Page

The Seal
Overview
Learn More
Apply Now
Tell a Merchant
Testimonials

Online Dispute Resolution
Overview
Learn More
File a Case
Respond to a Case
My Cases
Testimonials

Knowledge Center
Fraud Center
Success Story

Partners

ONVIA.com
Work. Wisely.™

About Us
Press Room
Mediators
Management
Advisors
Investors

Affiliate Program

Copyright 2000, SquareTrade, Inc.

Slide 4: Requesting a Mediator

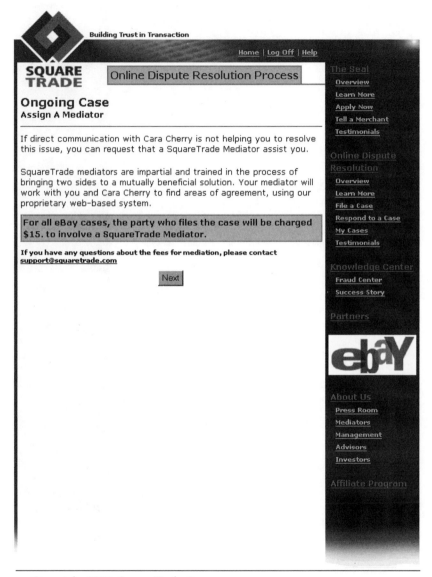

Slide 5: Resolution Achieved

SQUARE TRADE — Online Dispute Resolution Process

The following proposed resolution is awaiting your review:

This settlement agreement, agreed to on November 22, 2000 between Ms. Kristen Anderon and Ms. Cara Cherry Lisco, is intended to eliminate any obligations between the parties regarding any disputes between the parties arising from eBay transaction #384659119.

Both parties agree that in consideration of agreeing to this settlement, and Ms. Anderson returning the software to Ms. Lisco by Federal Express signature required, and by paying the cost for this return shipping, each party releases the other party from all liability for claims and/or demands which may arise from the transaction which is the subject of this agreement.

Both parties further agree that this settlement agreement is binding and shall be enforceable by any court of competent subject matter jurisdiction, and subject to the law of that jurisdiction.

Finally, both parties agree that this settlement agreement, and any communications confirming its acceptance, shall be confidential except as necessary to implement its terms or to enforce these terms in Court.

The parties acknowledge that they have voluntarily entered into this settlement agreement and that this writing constitutes the entire agreement between the parties pertaining to the subject matter contained in it.

Please state whether you accept this resolution. If you and the other party both accept it, it will be a binding agreement. Type your name into the text field that corresponds to your choice. If you represent another entity please add "on behalf of" and indicate who you represent.

◉ I, [Cara Cherry Lisco] accept this agreement on November 20, 2000 at 13:25:32 Pacific Time.

○ I, [Cara Cherry Lisco] choose to continue mediation on November 20, 2000 at 13:25:32 Pacific Time.

If you choose to continue mediation, please explain why below. The information will be sent to your mediator for response.

Navigation menu:
The Seal — Overview, Learn More, Apply Now, Tell a Merchant, Testimonials
Online Dispute Resolution — Overview, Learn More, File a Case, Respond to a Case, My Cases, Testimonials
Knowledge Center — Fraud Center, Success Story
Partners

About Us — Press Room, Mediators, Management, Advisors, Investors
Affiliate Program

Copyright 2000, SquareTrade, Inc.

Appendix 5:
Online Ombuds Office
Dispute Transcript

The Web Site Developer and the Newspaper

One of the unanticipated by-products of online mediation is the existence of a transcript of exchanges and communications among the participants. What follows is the transcript* of the Online Ombuds Office's first dispute in the Summer of 1996. This dispute is discussed earlier in the book on pp. 79–80. Even though we would have different tools to work with today, the transcript is useful for gaining an understanding of some of the novel challenges of mediating online.

This was a dispute between an individual and a newspaper. The individual had created a site on the World Wide Web that provided local news. Some of the material on his Web site consisted of summaries of news stories that appeared in the newspaper. The newspaper was alerted to the Web site, and some conversations took place between the individual and an editor of the paper. These conversations left the individual feeling threatened, and he temporarily took down his site and contacted us.

This dispute was instructive to us in a number of ways:

1. We were very fortunate in having this particular case as our first one. The parties were cooperative, reasonable, and amenable to

*Note: Transcripts are verbatim, but all identities have been disguised.

compromise. The dispute involved misinterpretations, misunderstandings, and miscommunications rather than competition over a scarce resource. We heard from the complainant fairly early in the dispute when the respondent's position had not yet hardened. While a more complex dispute might have provided more insight into how to mediate large-scale disputes online, this dispute did involve two core legal issues of cyberspace: rights of expression and rights of intellectual property. It revealed to us something about the then-existing state of the online environment, about how disputes were likely to arise online, and about concerns that online mediators needed to be aware of. It suggested to us that many disputes were likely to derive from misunderstandings linked to inexperience with the online environment, from contact with persons entering domains that previously were restricted, and from information distribution and processing capabilities that cost a fraction of what they had cost in the past. It also appeared to have been a learning experience for the newspaper and it made the paper more clearly aware of the Web environment. Less than a month after the dispute was resolved, the newspaper's own Web site appeared.

2. This dispute made it very clear to us that disputants we would come in contact with were likely to have very different levels of familiarity with cyberspace, and as a result, cases might, at times, involve some use of traditional media. Our individual complainant was clearly more savvy about the online world than the respondent newspaper and even appeared to have more online resources. Our one telephone conversation with the complainant took place because it was easier to obtain a large amount of information from him quickly via the phone. The two telephone conversations with the newspaper, however, were more a result of that being the most comfortable medium for the person involved.

3. It is important to be very sensitive to and realistic about the issues of time and speed. The new media have the potential to

assist rapid intervention, but there are also many factors that can interrupt or slow down the process. It is not necessarily true that the Internet will automatically accelerate dispute resolution. What is most likely is that if we wish to expedite dispute resolution, we will be able to do so, but only if we are much more focused on methods of saving time.

4. Much time was spent contacting the respondent and securing its cooperation. This has been a challenge in many of the cases presented to us. Originally, this process of contacting the respondent seemed to us to represent a premediation or intake phase. It may, however, just as easily be considered the first phase of mediation where the process is explained, ground rules are laid out, and the tone for future conversations is set. In the electronic environment, the boundary between intake and mediation may blur even more than it sometimes does in the physical world. All communication online takes place in the same place and some cues that suggest different stages of a process are lacking.

5. It was highly beneficial that the mediators had a sophisticated understanding of the online environment. The ability to understand the dispute and facilitate resolution was enhanced, it seems to us, by awareness of the online context. Knowledge of the Web was important in understanding the power relationship between individual and newspaper, the potential for widespread embarrassment to the newspaper, the ability to keep in close contact with the complainant, the ability of the complainant to move his site "underground," and the ability to use Web search engines to find information about the parties.

6. The parties here were not brought together face to face even though they were in the same area and a physical meeting was possible. One of our premises of online intervention was that it would be employed because parties were separated by distance. Here, only the mediators were at a distance. We had not anticipated this situation, and, in this particular case,

nothing was lost by not bringing the parties together. In an appropriate case of this type, however, use of a local mediator might be considered.

7. At one point in the mediation, we asked an assistant to see if he could find some information on the Web about the parties. The Web allows one to find information about disputants in ways that are generally not possible offline. Although we did this in this dispute, we usually do not use the Web in this manner, preferring instead to rely on the information provided by the parties. We are aware that in some of the ICANN domain name arbitrations, arbitrators do look up information about the number of domain names a party might have registered or some other information relevant to the dispute. In that context, we do not see any problem. What is clear is that as information becomes even more accessible online than it is now, for example, we might be able to find out whether some online seller has been involved in many other disputes, and this will become an issue that will need to be examined carefully.

Chronology of the Dispute and Transcript of Mediation Process:

- **July 14, 1996**

  — Complaint

- **July 16, 1996**

  — Response to complaint

  — Message from complainant

- **July 17, 1996**

  — Message from complainant

  — Research about respondent

  — Message to complainant

  — Message from complainant

  — Message to complainant

- **July 18, 1996**
  - Request for phone call
  - Telephone call to complainant

- **July 19, 1996**
  - Research about respondent

- **July 22, 1996**
  - ISP message
  - Message to complainant
  - Message from complainant
  - Message to complainant

- **July 23, 1996**
  - Message from newspaper
  - Telephone conversation with Jessica Dent
  - Fax to Somerset Union Journal editor
  - Message to complainant
  - Message from complainant
  - Message to complainant
  - Message from complainant
  - Message to complainant

- **July 26, 1996**
  - Message to complainant

- **July 31, 1996**
  - Message to complainant
  - Telephone conversation with newspaper
  - Telephone conversation with newspaper

- **August 9, 1996**
  - Message to complainant
  - Message from complainant

- **August 13, 1996**
  — Memo to complainant and respondent
  — Message from complainant

Date: Sun, 14 Jul 1996 21:41:53 -0400
From: Robert Gray rgray@provider.net
To: ombuds@titan.oit.umass.edu
Subject: I tried to send this else where, but it came back!

Hello. .

I am a computer hobbist, and found a void that I thought that I could fill on the net. I am from Hampshire County, Kansas and decided to publish the news from the area. I come home from work . . read the paper, listen to the radio and watch the local television newscast and with all that . . summarize the dailey news and events and publish this on the web at: http://www.provider.net/ HampshireCountyNews

A few weeks ago, I was contacted by the local print media that I am in violation of copyright infringement and that I must stop immeadiatly . . they also accused me of making money through this . . which I don't.

heard different opinions from the right to fair comment to *%#@ them!

What I have done . . . while awaiting what my next move will be is to chop up the news even more . . it's like a third grader wrote it. I have many different people who have wrote in support of what I am doing. BTW.they also said that I was pre-empting a business oppertunity, which I feel is the real reason they want me to quite. The have an email address, but DO NOT have a web site!

Thank You . .

Robert Gray34 Elms RoadSomerset, Kansas
***

Date: Tue, 16 Jul 1996 16:07:01 -0400 (EDT)
From: "Ethan Katsh" <katsh@titan.oit.umass.edu>
To: Rgray@provider.net (Robert Gray)
Subject: Re: Online Ombuds Office

Thanks for contacting us. If we can be of assistance, we would be happy to do so. I should reiterate that we are not a court and cannot order anyone to do anything. We do have experts who could assist you and your adversary to settle your differences but a willingness of the other side to participate is necessary. We would be happy to contact the print newspaper, if you wish us to do so, and can provide us with their email address. It is not easy to predict whether they would be willing to cooperate but I would hope that they would see the value of doing so in a case like this.

It would also be helpful to us to know more about how long you have been summarizing the news and what, specifically, they objected to. I did look at your Web site briefly and it did not appear to me that you were taking the whole paper. Do you think that they understand what it is you have done or do they appear to be relying on what someone has told them? Have you responded in any way to them? In other words, the more detail you can provide us about your activities, the better position we would be in if were are able to intervene. By the way, nothing that you tell us would be transmitted to the other side without your consent. We try to insure that this process is confidential.

Thank you again for contacting us.

Ethan Katsh

***

Date: Tue, 16 Jul 1996 22:38:33 -0400
From: Robert Gray rgray@provider.net
To: Ethan Katsh <katsh@legal.umass.edu>
Subject: Re: Online Ombuds Office

Hello . .

Thanks for your response. To answer some of your questions . . . First, I have been doing this since March of 1996 and the site that you looked at is the result of 2 discussions that we had. It was more detailed . . names, places and happenings. but they scared me with a lawsuit. They objected to the whole concept . . stating that I was copyrighting thier material, plagerizing thier work and pre-empting a bussiness opportunity for them. They came accross my site when they got thier internet account form the ISP. I contacted them to explain this and the editor flatly refused to negotiate anything. Her words were "you are copyrighting our paper and I would recommend that you quite or we will have to take necessary action". I believe that thier email address is: uj@provider.net, if that is not correct please contact me and I will get the correct one!!!

Thanks again . .

Robert Gray536 Elms Rd Somerset, Kansas

***

Date: Wed, 17 Jul 1996 23:50:10 -0400
From: Robert Gray <rgray@provider.net>
To: Ethan Katsh <katsh@legal.umass.edu>
Subject: Re: Online Ombuds Office

Ethan . . .

Please take your time . . just as long as what is done is of the best quality is all that I ask . . . kinda like representation with class!:))

I can get all the info you need, but I think a phone call could clear most of it up! We need to set that up! I havn't talked to the Somerset Union Journal for about a month now!

Well talk later!!

***

Date: Wed, 17 Jul 1996 12:31:28 -0400 (EDT)
From: "Ethan Katsh" <katsh@titan.oit.umass.edu>
To: bdelong (B.K. DeLong)
Subject: Gray Dispute

Ben -

Can you find out some information about provider.net and whether there is anything on the net about the newspaper in this dispute (its address may be uj@provider.net) Also, take a look at http://www.provider.net/HampshireCountyNews. Does it look like a newspaper to you?

Ethan

***

Date: Wed, 17 Jul 1996 12:38:02 -0400 (EDT)
From: "Ethan Katsh" <katsh@titan.oit.umass.edu>
To: rgray@provider.net (Robert Gray)
Subject: Re: Online Ombuds Office

Ron -

I hope that you do not mind a few more questions. I am curious what the name of the paper is (are they concerned that your readers might be confusing you with the paper? Is the name something like Hampshire County News?), whether there are other competing papers, and how much you changed your web site after speaking with the paper. If you have any written letters or messages from them, can you send them to me or fax them? If all communication was over the phone, how many calls were there and who, specifically, did you speak to? Also, I notice that you and the paper seem to use the same ISP. Has the ISP been contacted at all in this dispute and does it have any position? It would also be helpful to see a copy of the paper. If you could send me a copy in the mail, I'd appreciate it.
Ethan Katsh

***

Date: Wed, 17 Jul 1996 13:04:53 -0400
From: Robert Gray <Rgray@provider.net
To: Ethan Katsh <katsh@legal.umass.edu>
Subject: Re: Online Ombuds Office

Hello . .

I have no problem answering any questions . . the name of the Newspaper is the "Somerset Union Journal" and there are 2 other competing papers but they are more distant with our area news . . . both are outside 20 miles from here!

To give you an idea if how I use to write the page, (please do not repaeat this) it is my underground page that I sent my readers who emailed me To: http://www.underground.com/gray/secret.html This is exactly how is use to be written.

All communication has been over the phone 3 phone calls were made from me . . to the editor . . I forgot her name, she had contacted the ISP to find out who I was and why I was doing it . . they gave no information, but he contacted me and advised me of this . . that is when I contacted the paper! The ISP says that they do not hold a posistion! As far as they are concerned as long as I am paying . . I can do as I please!

I made a phone call to you just a bit ago and now have to leave for work . . so if there is anything further . . just email me and I will respond ASAP!!

Thanks

Robert Gray

***

Date: Wed, 17 Jul 1996 13:24:34 -0400 (EDT)
From: "Ethan Katsh"<katsh@titan.oit.umass.edu>
To: Rgray@provider.net (Robert Gray)
Subject: Re: Online Ombuds Office

Your ISP sounds pretty enlightened. I would still like to see a copy of the paper. Can you give me the name of the editor you spoke to. Was there more than one? Do you recall what the three conversations were about and how far apart they were? When was the last conversation?

Can you give me a sense of how fast you need to have this settled? I have no problem with trying to reach the people at the paper but it would also be helpful to me, for a variety of reasons, to wait until early next week. It is really up to you and your needs and wishes.

Ethan Katsh

***

Date: Thu, 18 Jul 1996 10:35:08 -0400
From: Robert Gray<Rgray@provider.net>
To: Ethan Katsh <katsh@legal.umass.edu>
Subject: Re: Online Ombuds Office

Hello . .

Just got your message, I am off today from work.so if you would please call me at your convience at . .
Thanks . .

Rob

Telephone Call to Complainant

Summary of telephone conversation: Mr. Gray explained that, several weeks earlier, he had three telephone conversations with the editor of the Somerset Union-Journal. These conversations left him feeling that he might be sued by the paper if he continued to maintain his Web site. His recollection was that the editor had asked him to stop and had claimed that this was a competing business to the paper. She alleged that he was also out to make money from this activity by putting advertisements on the Web site. Gray indicated that he did have one link to a local radio station but insisted that he was not engaged in a commercial activity and the radio link was only done because he liked the radio station.

Gray said that he found the editor's tone quite threatening and that he also was disturbed by a fax he received. This fax suggested to him that indeed the newspaper was concerned about his Web activity and had discussed with his Internet service provider the possibility of a copyright action.

[Editor's note: The fax referred to above was a fax from the Internet Service Provider to both Mr. Gray and the newspaper. Part of the dispute here might be traced to the fact that both parties used the same Internet Service Provider. The fax was apparently sent by the Internet Service Provider on its own when it became aware of what Mr. Gray was doing. Mr. Gray, however, appears to have interpreted the fax as coming at the instigation of the newspaper and saw it not as a reminder of the rules of copyright but as a warning that what he was doing could be perceived as being a violation of copyright law. What the fax simply contained was a document called "Ten Big Myths About Copyright Explained".]

***

Date: Fri, 19 Jul 1996 11:24:05 -0400
From: "B.K. DeLong" <bdelong@oitunix.oit.umass.edu>
To: katsh@oitunix.oit.umass.edu
Subject: Info on Somerset Union Journal

Found this on Lexis this morning:
    Somerset Union Journal1430 MainStreet Somerset, Kansas Simon ChasePublisher

—

B.K. DeLong ('98) Webmaster ***

***

Date: Mon, 22 Jul 1996 11:24:40 -0400 (EDT)
From: "Frank P. Glenn" <fpg@provider.net>
To: "Somerset Union Journal (Simon Chase)"
<uj@provider.net>
Cc: ETHAN KATSH <katsh@legal.umass.edu>
Subject: Help (fwd)
——Forwarded message——

Date: Mon, 22 Jul 1996 11:14:08 -0400
From: ETHAN KATSH <katsh@legal.umass.edu>
To: support@provider.net
Cc: katsh@legal.umass.edu
Subject: Help

Hi

I hope that you can help me. I was told that the Union Journal in Somerset had an email address of uj@provider.net. I want to contact one of their editors but was unclear whether this is the paper's address or just some individuals. Can you help me with this? Many thanks.

Ethan Katsh University of Massachusetts

***

Date: Mon, 22 Jul 1996 15:11:47 -0400 (EDT)
From: "Ethan Katsh" <katsh@titan.oit.umass.edu>
To: Rgray@provider.net (Robert Gray)
Subject: Contacting the paper

Ron -

Just wanted to let you know that we are working on getting in touch with the paper. This may turn out to take a little longer than we would like, partly because it is summer but mostly because I think we will have to resort to something other than email. My experience with newspapers is that, in general, they are not really familiar with the Net. The email address you gave me is their address but no one has yet replied, so I think phone and fax will be necessary. (When you spoke with Ms. Marshall, did she seem to have any familiarity with the Web?)

If you think of anything else that might be useful, let me know.

Ethan Katsh

***

Date: Mon, 22 Jul 1996 15:57:18 -0400
From: Robert Gray <Rgray@provider.net>

To: Ethan Katsh <katsh@legal.umass.edu>
Subject: Re: Contacting the paper

Thanks for advising me . . I was just sitting here wondering what was going on! Well, Ms Marshall did not seem at all like she was aware of the web. Because as you remember it came down a couple of days after the CDA was repealled and it gave almost a free for all on the net.

She made no comment on that or the repercussions that it could have on them or me. I really feel that thier next angle will be plagerism. Because they can't use copyright infringement because . . . it's like me doing a book report, I read and summarize what I read. The one thing that irrates me is that they think that I use only thier paper and thier news! That is totally wrong! In any story from Amsterdam/Bergholz/E.Springfield, comes from the source . . whichh at times I may wait to read what the Somerset Union Journal has printed then write it, information from Somerset is my own knowledge . . I live here and the Somerset and few other areas, I use the radio, TV and 2 other papers.
So thats it in a nut shell!!

Thanks again and as always,

GOD BLESS

Rob

***

Date: Mon, 22 Jul 1996 16:16:51 -0400 (EDT)
From: "Ethan Katsh" <katsh@titan.oit.umass.edu>
To: Rgray@provider.net (Robert Gray)
Subject: Re: Contacting the paper

Rob -
    We are so used to everything happening so fast on the Internet that delays sometimes seem unreasonable. I will keep you up to date on what is happening (even when nothing is happening). By

the way, I generally resist giving anyone legal advice but you should be aware that plagiarism is not a crime. In our schools, we certainly tell people not to plagiarize, and it may sometimes be the wrong thing to do, but the law only deals with copyright, not plagiarism.

Ethan

***

Date: Tue, 23 Jul 1996 11:07:39 -0500 (EST)
From: The Somerset Union Journal <uj@provider.net>
To: katsh@legal.umass.edu
Subject: Somerset Union Journal

Hi, Ethan.

I'm Jessica Dent, metro editor for the Somerset Union Journal and The Daily Times. i'm returning email you sent to our provider service regarding our addresses. Stephanie is out of the office this week so i'm finally returning your message. sorry it took so long. you can send email to Stephanie directly at editor @provider.net. the uj@provider.net address is sort of our internal/personal mailbox we set up as we were building our network of boxes. we're still in the progress of building this up. anything you send to any of our addresses will get to her because we're small. we just tell each other when someone receives mail in a different box. we're in the process of building a website. i noticed the word "legal" in your address. we're discussing libel on the internet and content issues before the page is officially online. if you have any advice, we'd be grateful.

Jessica Dent Somerset Union Journal and The Daily Times

Telephone Conversation with Jessica Dent, July 22, 1996

Ethan Katsh had a brief conversation with Jessica Dent to explain the reason for his email and to find out who at the newspaper would be the appropriate person to approach about the dispute. Ms. Dent indicated that she was aware of Mr. Gray but that the conversations with Mr. Gray had been with the paper's editor, Stephanie Marshall. Ms. Marshall was on vacation and would not be back until the next week. Katsh indicated that he would fax some information to the paper concerning the Online Ombuds Office and its approach in resolving disputes.

***

Fax to Somerset Union Journal Editor, July 23, 1996

Dear Ms. Dent:

I appreciated being able to speak with you this morning. How the Internet works and what happens there can seem a little strange so I thought that I might explain how I came to contact you. Please pass this on to Ms. Marshall or whomever I will be in further contact with.

I am a professor of legal studies at the University of Massachusetts and serve as co-director of the Online Ombuds Office, a project that was recently established to try to mediate disputes that occur as a result of online activities. We have received considerable media attention in the last three weeks, including articles in the online New York Times (http://www.nytimes.com/library/cyber/week/0714ombuds.html) and the Wall Street Journal (http://interactive3.wsj.com/edition/current/articles/SB8332979927 27904000.htm). If you have access to a World Wide Web browser, you can obtain more information about us at http://www.ombuds.org.

Recently, we were contacted by Mr. Robert Gray, who lives in your area. Mr. Gray informed us that, a few weeks ago, he had spoken to you several times about his World Wide Web site. On this site, he provided news about your area. Some of the stories on the site consisted of summaries of stories that appeared in your newspaper.

Mr. Gray indicated that you believed that his activity might be infringing on copyrights that you hold. He, on the other hand, is concerned that certain First Amendment rights of his to publish are at stake here. Indeed, he has removed some content from his site due to discussions with you. Because of this, he asked us if we might discuss with you how the concerns of each of you might be satisfied.

My purpose in writing is to ask whether you would be willing to participate in an online mediation with us and Mr. Gray to see whether this disagreement might be resolved to the satisfaction of both of you. I emphasized to Mr. Gray, and I repeat here, that we are not a court or a group of judges that makes rulings about who is right and who is wrong. We do not declare winners and losers. We would provide, free of charge, an experienced mediator who might make some suggestions and take other steps to facilitate an agreement. (We are a pilot project funded by the National Center for Information Research to experiment with online dispute resolution techniques). As is true with mediation generally, you have nothing to lose since, if you feel that Mr. Gray is unreasonable, you do not have to agree to anything.

The only other quality of the process that I would mention is that we endorse confidentiality. This is a dispute between your paper and Mr. Gray. We are a neutral and, unless we received your permission to do so, would not reveal any information about the content of our discussions. I would think that this is certainly a preferable method of resolving a dispute than allowing word to leak out onto the Net where sensitivity about publishing on the web is high, where rumor circulates as fast as fact, and where setting the record straight, after the fact, borders on the impossible. This particular dispute is one which the Net community would, I believe, find of particular interest.

If you are unfamiliar with the Internet, my proposal may sound a little strange. I would be happy to speak to you on the phone about this, if you so desire.
Thank you very much for your cooperation.

***

Date: Tue, 23 Jul 1996 11:39:36 -0400 (EDT)
From: "Ethan Katsh" <katsh@titan.oit.umass.edu>

To: Rgray@provider.net (Robert Gray)
Subject: Re: Contacting the paper

Ron -

I just wanted to let you know that I have had a telephone conversation with one of the editors at the Somerset Union Journal. Ms. Marshall is on vacation this week and the person I spoke to thought I should probably speak with her. They were, aware of you, however. If you don't mind, therefore, there may not be any progress until Ms. Marshall gets back next week. The only tidbit I did gain from them is that they are planning to have a Website of some kind. I have no idea, however, what their time frame is. Can you let me know how often your Web site was revised and how many stories, approximately, you might include each day?

Ethan

***

Date: Tue, 23 Jul 1996 14:49:21 -0400
From rgray@provider.net Tue Jul 23 14:48:56 1996
To: Ethan Katsh <katsh@legal.umass.edu>
Subject: Re: Contacting the paper

Ethan . . . .

That doesn't sound good . . "they are aware" of me! But anyhow, my site is update usally as events warrant . . so if a few days go bye and there is really no . . "county" issues or news, then it is not updated . . . .but, as a practice . . . I update dailey and the average amount of stories are about 2-3 per day . . . remember though I don't put in little stupid stuff! Only stories that may affect a number of people . . . which readers want to know about! BTW . . . I havn't recieved thier paper in over a week . . so that may go to show you how childish this can get. They have yet to give me a reason for not delivering the paper to me.

Well . . . I guess it's just wait and see!

—

Thanks and as always . . . .

GOD BLESS

***

Date: Tue, 23 Jul 1996 15:00:38 -0400 (EDT)
From: "Ethan Katsh" <katsh@titan.oit.umass.edu>
To: rgray@provider.net (Robert Gray)
Subject: Re: Contacting the paper
>
> Ethan . . . .> That dosn't sound good . . "they are aware" of me!
But anyhow, my site is
    Actually, I don't think it means anything and I would guess that
no one has been looking recently at your stuff. All I meant was that
the person who I spoke to had heard something about a Web site
that had local stories and I did not have to provide a lengthy introduction.
    If you can remember when you get your paper (if you ever do
get another paper) to send me a copy, I would be interested in seeing it.
Thanks.

Ethan

***

Date: Tue, 23 Jul 1996 16:10:01 -0400
From: Robert Gray <Rgray@provider.net>
To: Ethan Katsh <katsh@legal.umass.edu>
Subject: Got one!!!

OK!!
    I did recieve a paper today!! I will attempt to get it to you
quickly! I have advised readers on the underground area . . . that I

feel that this may be leading to the end of my part, because they seem as though they will get on the net quickly!

I do need two things from you: 1) what does OMBUDS stand for and 2) a link that I can use for readers who would like to chek out your site!! and a summation of exactly what you do! (that'll help)

***

Date: Tue, 23 Jul 1996 17:39:18 -0400 (EDT)
From: "Ethan Katsh" <katsh@titan.oit.umass.edu>
To: Rgray@provider.net (Robert Gray)
Subject: Re: Got one!!!

OK!!

I did recieve a paper today!! I will attempt to get it to you quickly! > I have advised readers on the underground area . . . that I feel that this > may be leading to the end of my part, because they seem as though they > will get on the net quickly!

I'd like to take credit for your getting the newspaper but I think the delay is only the fault of the mail. Seriously, I would make a request that my involvement here not be mentioned until we actually have an agreement that is satisfactory to you. We don't know when the paper will be on the Net and the fewer people who know about your problems with the paper, the easier it will probably be to get this resolved quickly. Obviously, some of your readers may already be aware of what happened. I just wouldn't publicize it any more, for the time being.

I certainly do not mind your linking to our site http://www.ombuds.org and indicating that we are prepared to intervene in disputes that arise out of online activities and that there is no charge for our service. Ombuds is actually short for ombudsman or ombudsperson. It is a Swedish word for someone who intervenes in disputes.

Ethan

***

Date: Fri, 26 Jul 1996 12:55:34 -0400 (EDT)
From: "Ethan Katsh" <katsh@titan.oit.umass.edu>
To: Rgray@provider.net (Robert Gray)
Subject: Re: Online Ombuds Office

Rob -

I just wanted to let you know that there is nothing new and that I have to be away, probably until Tuesday. Since Ms. Marshall is not back from vacation until Monday, I don't think this matters. I do hope that I can communicate with her when I return and get some clearer information about what their concerns and intentions are. Best regards.

Ethan

***

Date: Wed, 31 Jul 1996 19:09:56 -0400 (EDT)
From: "Ethan Katsh" <katsh@titan.oit.umass.edu>
To: Rgray@provider.net (Robert Gray)
Subject: Re: dispute

Rob-

I've been away since the beginning of the week and have not received any further communication from the paper. We will spend the next few days trying to contact the paper and persuade them that they should participate in discussions about your concerns. Getting their agreement to participate is obviously critical and sometimes takes a little longer than one might like. I'll let you know as soon as we hear something more definite.
Ethan

Telephone Conversation with Newspaper, August 1, 1996

Janet Rifkin, Co-director of the Online Ombudspeople involved in this case, spoke with Stephanie Marshall, the Editor of the paper.

Rifkin explained who she was, what the Online Ombuds Office was, and summarized the complainant's issues with the paper. Rifkin explored with Marshall her understanding of both the circumstances that gave rise to Gray's complaint as well as Marshall's understanding of some of the potential legal implications. Marshall explained that she and others at the paper had originally felt that Gray might have been posting verbatim news accounts from their paper and from no other sources. She had since learned that his Web site consisted of postings which summarized news from a number of sources. She also indicated that she understood that he was within his First Amendment rights to engage in these activities and that her Paper had no desire or intent to stop him. She did indicate that the paper would be posting its own Web site in the early fall and was glad to hear that this would satisfy Gray's major concern. Although she preferred that Gray discontinue publishing his Web site, which he indicated he would do if the paper posted its own, she also indicated that the paper was not in the position, nor had any desire, to stop him from doing so.

In the course of the conversation, she expressed her concern that this dispute had developed as it did, and that she felt quite bad about causing Mr. Gray unnecessary distress. She speculated that the source of the problem stemmed from her having contacted the Internet service provider (ISP) when she discovered Gray's Web site, in an effort to clarify whether the paper had any legal concerns to protect. The Internet service provider, although not asked to do so, sent Gray a long message about copyright infringement. In retrospect, it was clear to her that Gray interpreted this message as a threat, assumed that the paper must have directed the ISP to act in this way, and anticipated that the paper was pursuing or contemplating legal action. In fact, nether Marshall or anyone else at the paper knew what had been sent, and when she saw the message she understood why Gray had reacted as he did. She wanted him to know that she apologized for causing him to worry. There was no indication from Marshall as to why her recollection of the telephone conversation with Gray differed considerably from his.

Telephone Conversation with Newspaper, August 8, 1996

This follow-up conversation between Janet Rifkin and Stephanie Marshall reviewed the conversation which they had the week before and confirmed the details of the agreement that had been reached.

Date: Fri, 09 Aug 1996
From: "Ethan Katsh" <katsh@titan.oit.umass.edu>
To: Rgray@provider.net (Robert Gray)
Subject: Congratulations

Rob-

I thought that I would send a quick note to you indicating that we have had several conversations with the newspaper and they do not have any plans to take any action regarding your Web site. I will prepare a a lengthier memo next week with more details but I thought that this would alleviate some of your anxieties . .

Good luck!

Ethan

***

Date: Fri, 09 Aug 1996 18:57:04 -0400
From: Robert Gray <Rgray@provider.net>
To: Ethan Katsh <katsh@legal.umass.edu>
Subject: Re: Congratulations!

Ethan . . .

I am beyond shocked!!! WOW!! I am really . . really suprised at this development . . . I honestly thought that we would of got no where with them.

Well, I can't wait to hear the details.

Thanks . . hope to talk to you soon!

Robert Gray

***

Date: Tue, 13 Aug 1996 13:57:58 -0400 (EDT)
From: "Ethan Katsh" <katsh@titan.oit.umass.edu>
To: Rgray@provider.net
Subject: Online dispute

Rob -

Attached is the memo I am sending to you and Stephanie Marshall. What it boils down to is that they have no problem with your putting your Web site back up if you do not copy words and language from their stories. We request that you not publicize the dispute (although if you want to put a link to us at http://www.ombuds.org and indicate that you find us a useful service, that would be gratefully appreciated). Other than that, if you have any questions about any of this please feel free to write.

Ethan

***

To: Stephanie Marshall and Robert Gray
From: Ethan Katsh, Online Ombuds Office
Subject: Robert Gray's Web site

August 13, 1996

Janet Rifkin will be out of the country for the next two weeks and, before leaving, she asked me to summarize some of the conversations that took place recently concerning Mr. Robert Gray's World Wide Web site.

Several months ago, Mr. Gray created a Web site that, among other things, provided news of interest to inhabitants of Hampshire County, Kansas. Mr. Gray provided access without charge to users. Nor did he charge for what appeared to be advertisements on the site. This Web site came to the attention of the Somerset Union Journal and was the subject of several conversations between Mr. Gray and Ms. Stephanie Marshall, Editor of the Somerset Union Journal. The Web site was also the subject of at least one message from Provider.net, the Internet service provider for both Gray and the Somerset Union Journal. A representative of Provider.net supplied both parties with a copy of a list of rules related to copyright infringement that had been posted on the Internet.

Mr. Gray contacted the Online Ombuds Office because he felt that the newspaper objected to his site and, possibly, might even entertain taking legal action. The Somerset Union Journal, while concerned over the possibility that Mr. Gray might use actual stories and language from the newspaper, and whatever the nature of the conversations between Mr. Gray and Ms. Marshall, never initiated any steps to challenge what Mr. Gray was doing.

The Somerset Union Journal is still primarily concerned that Mr. Gray not use verbatim copies of Somerset Union Journal stories. It does not appear that Mr. Gray has ever used verbatim stories and he has stated to us that it is not his intention to do so. Mr. Gray has also used information from sources other than the Somerset Union Journal and expects to continue doing so in the future. Under such circumstances, the Somerset Union Journal has no intention to pursue legal action.

Mr. Gray has stated that his main concern is providing access to local information on the World Wide Web. The Somerset Union Journal intends to create its own Web site in the Fall. Mr. Gray has stated that such a site with local information may make his own site unnecessary and that, if the Somerset Union Journal site satisfies his concerns for local Web news, he would discontinue his own local coverage at that time.

We have been impressed with the willingness of both parties to discuss this dispute with us. There were a variety of misunderstandings but there appears to us to have also been good faith on both sides. If any problems between the parties arise in the future, we would urge them to contact us. In addition, we urge both parties not to publicize this dispute. Privacy is often helpful in resolving disputes and there is little to be gained by publicity at this time.

Thank you again for your cooperation.

***

Date: Tue, 13 Aug 1996 14:34:23 -0400
From: rgray@provider.net
To: Ethan Katsh <katsh@legal.umass.edu>
Subject: Re: Online dispute

Ethan . . .

This apears to be a major breakthough . . considering past conversations with the Somerset Union Journal . . . I am pleased with the fact that they have agreed to be more lienient with there restrictions . . . .as nothing could be gained otherwise.

I am saying at this point that I have no objections to thier request and that I honor thier concerns and will standby this aggreement!!

Thank you for a job well done!

Notes

Introduction

1 A more detailed analysis of the eBay project can be found in Katsh, Rifkin, and Gaitenby, "E-Commerce, E-Disputes, and E-Dispute Resolution: In the Shadow of 'eBay Law,'" *Ohio State Journal of Dispute Resolution*, 15(3), 705–734 (2000) [http://www.umass.edu/cyber/katsh.pdf]

2 Katsh, E., "The Online Ombuds Office: Adapting Dispute Resolution to Cyberspace" (1996) [http://mantle.sbs.umass.edu/vmag/disres.html]

3 http://www.icann.org

4 http://www.umass.edu/dispute

5 http://www.umass.edu/cyber

6 http://www.icann.org/udrp/udrp.htm

7 http://www.squaretrade.com

8 http://www.clicknsettle.com

9 http://www.cybersettle.com

Chapter One

1 http://archives.obs-us.com/obs/english/books/nn/ch01c01.htm

2 McLuhan, M., *Understanding Media*. New York: McGraw-Hill, 1964. p. 161.

3 609 F. Supp. 1307 (E.D. Pa, 1985), aff'd 797 F.2d 1222 (3d Cir. 1986), cert. denied 479 U.S. 1031 (1987).

4 Kagel, S., and Kelly, K., "The Anatomy of Mediation: What Makes It Work." *J. Dis. Res.* 201 (1990).

5 See, for example, the Courtroom21 project [http://www.courtroom21.net].

6 See, for example, http://www.americounsel.com and http://www.mycounsel.com.

7 Margaret Wertheim, M., *The Pearly Gates of Cyberspace: A History of Space From Dante to the Internet.* New York: W. W. Norton and Co., 1999. p. 305.

Chapter Two

1 http://www.hcc.hawaii.edu/bdgtti/bdgtti-1.02_8.html#SEC62

2 MacDuff, I., "Flames on the Wire: Mediating from an Electronic Cottage." *10 Negotiation Journal* 5 (1994).

3 One can subscribe to dispute-res by sending a message to listserv@listserv.law.cornell.edu. The message should say "subscribe dispute-res yourfirstname yourlastname"

4 Van Gelder, L., "The Strange Case of the Electronic Lover." *Ms. Magazine*, 1985.

5 Dibble, J., "A Rape in Cyberspace." *The Village Voice*, 12/21/93, pp. 36–42 (1993) [http://www.levity.com/julian/bungle.html].

6 Holmes, O.W., *The Common Law.* Boston: Little, Brown, 1881. p. 5.

7 *United States of America v. Abraham Jacob Alkhabaz, also known as Jake Baker*, 104 F.3d 1492 (1997)

8 *United States v. LaMacchia*, 871 F. Supp. 535 (1994)

9 http://www.ftc.gov/opa/1999/9912/case121599.pdf

10 http://mantle.sbs.umass.edu/vmag/disres.html

11 http://www.vmag.org

12 http://mantle.sbs.umass.edu/vmag/granat.htm

13 http://www.ftc.gov/bcp/icpw/index.htm

14 http://www.ftc.gov/bcp/altdisresolution/index.htm

15 http://www.ftc.gov/bcp/altdisresolution/summary.htm

16 http://www.gbd.org

17 http://www.oecd.org and http://arbiter.wipo.int/events/conferences/2000/index.html

18 http://port4.com/dcforum/DCForumID3/20.html

19 http://www.smartsettle.com

20 http://tess.uspto.gov/bin/gate.exe?f=tess&state=nvbp56.1.1

21 http://www.icann.org/udrp/udrp.htm

22 http://www.squaretrade.com/learnmore/standards_092000.jsp

23 "The students had thought only 20 friends were receiving their email, but some campuses were listening so intently that computer systems crashed. Included in the list: 'If she can't speak, she can't cry rape.' According to Barbara Krause, judicial administrator for Cornell, Ithaca, N.Y., the four students will:

    • Attend Cornell's 'Sex at 7' program, which deals with date acquaintance rape.

    • Perform 50 hours of community service each. If possible, the work will be performed at a nonprofit agency whose primary focus relates to sexual assault or similar issues.

    • Meet with a group of Cornell senior administrators to apologize.

    Punishment options had ranged from apology to expulsion. Krause said she did not conclude that the students had engaged in sexual harassment because, she said, the target of their list was friends, and none of them had complained." Marco R. della Cava; Phillip Pina; Kim Painter, "Cornell punishes misogynist email." USA Today. November 21, 1995.

24 http://www.nua.ie/surveys/how_many_online/index.html

25 http://www.nua.ie/surveys/index.cgi?f=VS&art_id=905356259&rel=true

26 McDougall, P., "More Work Ahead—Yes, companies have embraced E-business. No, they haven't finished the job, says Gerstner." Information Week, December 18, 2000.

Chapter Three

1   See transcript in Appendix 5

2   http://aaron.sbs.umass.edu/center/ombuds/narrative1.html

3   Melamed, J., "What is Mediation"
    [http://mediate.com/articles/whatismediation.cfm]

4   Bourcier, D., Hassett, P., Roquilly, C., *Droit et Intelligence Artificielle*.
    Paris: Romillat, 2000. p. 20.

Chapter Four

1   http://www.bbb.org/alerts/bbbstats.asp;
    http://www.dr.bbb.org/news/comp-1999.cfm

2   Ethan Katsh, Janet Rifkin, and Alan Gaitenby, "E-Commerce,
    E-Disputes, and E-Dispute Resolution: In the Shadow of 'eBay
    Law'" *Ohio State Journal of Dispute Resolution*, 15(3), 705–734 (2000)
    [http://www.umass.edu/cyber/katsh.pdf]

3   Woerner, R., Beckers, S., Collier, M., *eBay for Dummies*. Foster City,
    CA: IDG Books Worldwide, 1999. p. 326.

Chapter Five

1   Macduff, I., "Flames on the Wires: Mediating from an Electronic
    Cottage." *10 Negotiation Journal 5*, (1994).

2   Grimaldi, J. V., "Microsoft, Justice Remain Far Apart; Sources Say
    Pact Unlikely by Tuesday." *Washington Post*, March 25, 2000. Pg. E1.

3   http://www.contuzzi.com

4   http://aaron.sbs.umass.edu/adronline2000/09/adronline.htm

Chapter Six

1   Tufte, E., *Envisioning Information*. Cheshire, CT: Graphics Press,
    1990. p. 121.

2 Hill, R., "Online Arbitration: Issues and Solutions," *Arbitration International*, April, 1999 [http://www.umass.edu/dispute/hill.htm]

3 http://www.disputes.net/cyberweek2000/tuefeb15.htm

4 Thompson, L., *The Mind and Heart of the Negotiator*. Upper Saddle River, NJ: Prentice Hall, 2001. 271–291.

5. Picard, C.A., *Mediation Skills*. Ottawa, Canada: The Mediation Centre at Carelton University, 1995.

About the Authors

Ethan Katsh is professor of legal studies and codirector of the Center for Information Technology and Dispute Resolution at the University of Massachusetts, Amherst. He is the author of *Law in a Digital World* (1995) and *The Electronic Media and the Transformation of Law* (1989). His articles have appeared in law reviews and law journals published by Yale, The University of Chicago, and other leading law schools.

Katsh is a graduate of the Yale Law School and for more than a decade has been involved in many law and technology projects. He is on the editorial board of *Cyberspace Law Abstracts*, is a fellow of the Cyberspace Law Institute, and is a nonresident scholar at the Chicago-Kent Law School Institute for Science, Law & Technology. His work has been supported by grants from the Hewlett Foundation, the Markle Foundation, the National Center for Automated Information Research, and the Massachusetts Foundation for the Humanities. He has assisted the Federal Trade Commission, the Department of Commerce, the Hague Conference on Private International Law, and the Internet Corporation for Assigned Names and Numbers (ICANN), and he lectures widely on law and Internet issues. He founded the Dispute-res listserv in 1994 and is a consultant to SquareTrade.com. He is reachable at Katsh@legal.umass.edu.

Janet Rifkin is Professor and Chair of the Legal Studies Department at the University of Massachusetts in Amherst. She is also the codirector of the university's Center for Information Technology and Dispute Resolution. She served as the University of Massachusetts Ombudsperson for five years. She has written numerous publications related to Alternative Dispute Resolution and she has conducted seminars, trainings, and workshops on mediation and dispute resolution throughout the United States and internationally.

She is a graduate of Sarah Lawrence College and New York University School of Law. She was the founder and director of the University Mediation Project, and cofounder of the National Association of Mediation and Education. She has served on the board of directors of several national organizations including the National Institute of Dispute Resolution, the National Conference on Peacemaking and Conflict Resolution, and she was an advisor to the ABA Special Committee on Dispute Resolution where she helped to train the first participants in the Multi-Door Courthouse program. She was the first recipient of the Margaret Hermann Founder's Award of the National Conference on Peacemaking and Conflict Resolution. She is a consultant to Squaretrade.com. She is reachable at jrifkin@legal.umass.edu

Index